Kelly McCants

at home with
modern june

27 Sewing Projects
for Your Handmade Lifestyle

stashBOOKS.

an imprint of C&T Publishing

Text copyright © 2014 by Kelly McCants

Photography and Artwork copyright © 2014 by C&T Publishing, Inc.

Publisher: Amy Marson

Creative Director: Gailen Runge

Art Director: Kristy Zacharias

Editor: S. Michele Fry

Technical Editors: Alison M. Schmidt and Gailen Runge

Cover/Book Designer: April Mostek

Production Coordinator: Zinnia Heinzmann

Production Editor: Joanna Burgarino

Illustrator: Wendy Mathson

Photo Assistant: Mary Peyton Peppo

Photography by Meghan McSweeney, unless othewise noted

Published by Stash Books, an imprint of
C&T Publishing, Inc., P.O. Box 1456, Lafayette, CA 94549

Library of Congress Cataloging-in-Publication Data

McCants, Kelly.

At home with Modern June : 27 sewing projects for your handmade lifestyle / Kelly McCants.

    pages cm

Includes bibliographical references.

ISBN 978-1-60705-800-7 (soft cover)

1. House furnishings. 2. Sewing. I. Modern June. II. Title.

TT387.M36 2014

645--dc23

                    2013030175

Printed in China

10 9 8 7 6 5 4 3 2 1

Dedication

This pretty book is for the people who share my cozy little home: Don, Maddie, and Aidan! Thank you all for the love you give to me every single day and for putting up with my creative madness. Most of all, thank you for helping make my dreams come true. I couldn't do it without you three.

Acknowledgments

I couldn't have made this book without the help of many wonderful people.

I work with some of the most amazing ladies in the world! I lovingly call them my Junies! Kathie, Geneva, and Nicole have grown to be family, and I love them very much. Thanks for rising to the occasion and having my back through the months of crazy and tight deadlines. Thanks for teaching me how to delegate.

I am forever grateful to the fine people at Stash Books and C&T Publishing for supporting this endeavor. It's been an honor to work with Roxane Cerda, Michele Fry, Kristy Zacharias, Alison Schmidt, and Zinnia Heinzmann. Thanks for helping publish this lovely book!

I am so happy that the talented photographer Meghan McSweeney made my home and all the projects in this book look so darn great! I am glad to call you friend. I'm so glad we got to work together again.

A special thanks goes out to all the companies that gave fabric, notions, and fluff to the cause: Wrights, Pellon, Moda Fabrics, Riley Blake, Fairfield, and Spoonflower. Working with their goods was fun and helpful!

CONTENTS

foreword

The week my first book, *Sewing with Oilcloth*, was published, Hurricane Irene bullied her way up the East Coast. On August 27, 2011, I sat in my home studio sewing the day away, all the while watching the 100-year-old oak tree in our backyard swing back and forth. Out that window I saw a transformer blow, and the explosion split a huge branch off a neighbor's walnut tree. At that point I was thankful that we still had power, and I joined my family for an evening of TV.

A few hours later, the old oak fell; it landed right on top of my studio and covered the entire back half of my house. I can't express how grateful I was that I was with my family and that all four of us were in one room—the living room, which is as far from the tree as possible. Best of all, we were fine!

The next day I went to my book release party in a state of shock while my husband tried to figure out what was next. Long story short, it took seven months and $70,000 to get our home back to normal. But I was determined early on to make lemonade from the lemons that the hurricane left behind.

Thanks to a very good insurance policy, we were getting more than half our home repaired, and you know what that means, don't you? New walls and ceilings mean new paint! Of course new paint means makeover! It wasn't long before I realized that I had the makings of a new book.

Join me as I put my sewing and patterning skills to work and make over my 87-year-old home! Whether you're moving into a new home, launching a whole home makeover, or just sprucing up one room at a time, I hope that this book inspires you as much as that tree did me!

xoxox, Kelly

introduction:

My Design Credo

When my husband and I were newlyweds, we spent an afternoon wandering a cool neighborhood in Baltimore, Maryland, with another young couple. We slowly looked through thrift, gift, and antique stores until we came upon a rug shop. The charming man who owned the store overheard me say that a particular kilim rug would match my new sofa perfectly, and he set out to teach me an important life lesson.

He insisted that *matching* was a bad word! Then to our surprise he shepherded us up the stairs to his home. There above the shop was a lifetime of treasures, an eclectic mix of everything that the man and his family had ever loved.

That day he told me to buy only the things I truly loved, and that in the end my home would work in perfect harmony. I've lived by this nontraditional design rule ever since, and I think it's worked out for me quite nicely.

I've kept a lot of tear sheets over the last ten to fourteen years, and the funny thing is, I still love most of them. Trends come and go, but if you go only for the ones that really speak to you, then they always fit in.

mood boards

Mood boards are amazing; they are a place for all your ideas to live. For me they hold an ever-changing assortment of visual goodness that helps guide me through my creative life. They can be very helpful to keep your home or work design projects inspired and on task.

My giant mood board hangs on the wall of my home studio. I use it for work and play! A mood board is an essential tool for me, so much so that I've shown you how to make one (page 141).

inspiration catch-all

For me a mood board spends most of its life as a feeling, as a mood. It's a place for all my little bits of inspiration to live—a color swatch that caught my eye, an outfit, or a home from a magazine. A photo of a stack of dishes that I saw at a junk shop but didn't need to buy. A printed picture from a beloved design blog. Fabric swatches—fabrics always find their way onto my board.

When the board is filled up with goodies, it becomes something real. If you keep these bits and pieces as life goes by, the design process is much easier. You don't have to think as hard when it's time to work.

board-inspired projects

I know it's time for a project when I start looking around the house and I think, "Meh!" I don't know about you, but if a project is too big, I have a hard time getting started; so I like to start small. I think *pillows*.

Pillows are always a great pick-me-up. You can use them inside and out to spruce up your living spaces and to inspire you to move on to bigger projects. Shopping from your mood board for fabric or a new color combination is a great place to start, isn't it? A trip to the fabric shop for a bit of fabric or an online order later, and you're ready to start to "make pretty."

project-based board

If you're making over an entire home as I did, you'll want a giant mood board divided into sections or a smaller board per room. This way the mood board can become more task specific.

At this point the board can include the fabric swatches, specs, floor plans, and paint chips for each room. The best thing is that it's all right there for you to see! It's like a functional art piece of its own.

terms and techniques glossary

fabrics

Batting: The inner layer of a quilt between the top and back; adds insulation and warmth. Usually cotton, wool, or polyester; gives the quilt its fluffiness and warmth. Newer types of batting are made from silk, cotton/polyester blends, soy fibers, and bamboo. Each type of batting material has different characteristics, giving dimension to the quilted surface.

Calico: A lightweight, woven cotton or cotton/polyester blend fabric with an allover print, usually a small floral pattern on a contrasting background color.

Canvas: A strong, durable, closely woven cotton fabric. Also called duck cloth.

Chalk cloth: A PVC-free fabric that is a bit thicker than oilcloth and less pliable. It is usually black, and you can write on it, just like a chalkboard.

Cotton: The cheapest and most available natural fiber, making it the most widely used fabric in the world. Cotton is durable and easy to clean, dyes well, and can be woven into a diverse number of products. Quilting cotton is usually 44" wide, but after prewashing and trimming selvages, consider it to have a usable width of 40".

Drapery, home decor fabric: These fabrics are created so you can mix and match patterns throughout a room. Coordinating styles include pretty prints, woven stripes and plaids, jacquards, solid textures. Look for a midweight fabric for curtains.

Feed sack: Until the mid-1900s, flour, sugar, salt, tobacco, and animal feed were sold in printed cloth sacks. Thrifty seamstresses would take the sacks apart and use the fabric for quilts and clothing.

Gingham: A medium-weight, plain-weave fabric with an even check pattern.

Laminated cotton: A high-quality cotton sheeting with a thin layer of polyurethane film adhered to the right side of the fabric, usually 56" wide. It's soft and has a very nice hand to it; it drapes very nicely. It's waterproof, durable, and easy to clean. Just don't iron the shiny side!

Linen or linen-blend fabric: Made from the flax plant, often loosely woven with a textured surface, and up to 55" wide.

Muslin: Inexpensive woven cotton that is usually not dyed. It's often used to test upholstery or garment patterns. It makes a great lining.

Oilcloth: A thick layer of PVC on top of a cotton mesh, 47" to 48" wide. It's waterproof, easy to clean, strong, and durable; oilcloth tablecloths remain bright and looking brand new for years and years.

Ticking: A closely woven cotton in a twill or satin weave, usually with woven stripes, and traditionally used for mattresses.

Twill: A fabric that shows a distinct diagonal wale on the face (for example, denim, gabardine, tricotine).

Upholstery fabric: Heavyweight, woven fabric for upholstery; stands up to long years of wear and is great for covering headboards, ottomans, or sofas. Widths vary but can be up to 60″.

Wool felt: Thick and durable fabric made with wool fibers that are matted together instead of woven. I prefer 100% wool felt—it has a spongier feel to it than the acrylic version.

tools

Beeswax: Coating thread with beeswax helps to keep the thread from tangling during hand sewing.

Clothespins: I find clothespins indispensable when working with oilcloth; they can be helpful when cutting and when topstitching a hem. These very clever gadgets keep you from getting pinholes in your projects. They also are helpful for keeping projects in order.

Cutting mat: A self-healing mat will protect your cutting surface when you use a rotary cutter.

Double-stick tape: To avoid pinning, a great trick is to use double-stick tape to hold material in place. I love to use it when appliquéing on oilcloth.

Dry-erase marker: A dry-erase marker is a great way to mark a line on oilcloth. You have to work quickly and make sure that you don't smear the line. Use a soft cloth to clean it off.

Embroidery floss or perle cotton: Floss is made up of six individual strands, and perle cotton is a tightly twisted two-strand thread. Both are great for embroidery. I prefer to use perle cotton for most of my handwork, but I save floss for stitches like the split stitch (page 173).

Embroidery hoops: Two concentric hoops that hold your fabric taut during embroidering to keep the weave of your fabric from becoming distorted.

Embroidery needles: These needles will glide through fabric smoothly and have a long eye for easier threading. They come in a variety of sizes; use a smaller needle on finer fabric, saving the thicker needles for sturdier material like felt.

Embroidery scissors or snips: I couldn't live without a pair of snips—they are very helpful for ripping out stitches, for cutting threads, and for making small or delicate details.

Fabric shears: I use regular fabric scissors for cutting all my fabrics. I do find that scissors dull faster when I cut a lot of oilcloth; I suggest using a new pair of inexpensive paper-cutting scissors for oilcloth projects.

Measuring tape: A strong, flexible, plastic-coated measuring tape is a constantly used tool throughout all sewing projects.

Needle threader: This is a very helpful tool for working with multiple strands of embroidery floss or thick perle cotton. To use, slip the flexible wire loop through the eye of the needle, feed the thread through it, and pull the wire and thread back out.

Paper-cutting scissors: It's best to keep a pair of good paper-cutting scissors at hand when sewing; this will keep you from using your good fabric shears on paper and packaging.

Pattern paper: I like the heavy-duty brown paper that you can buy at the hardware store. It's typically used to protect floors, so it's hardy enough to withstand frequent use as a pattern.

Pencils and pens: I usually use pencils, but occasionally I use a pen. Pens can show through oilcloth over time, so I *never* use a pen in the center of a project. I only use pen if the mark will be covered by cotton trim or encased in a seam. Pens can be helpful when you are drawing on chalk cloth. If you get ink on the right side of oilcloth, a bit of hair spray and a rag should save the day.

Pinking shears: Scissors with a sawtooth edge instead of a straight blade. Pinking shears cut fabric with a zigzag to keep it from fraying.

Pins: I use traditional dressmaking pins for most of my projects, but occasionally I find quilting pins to be helpful if I am going through something thick. They are easier to push in and pull out. Refer to *pinning oilcloth* (page 16, in Tips and Tricks) for more on pinning oilcoth.

Roller or Teflon foot: These specialty feet have rollers or a Teflon coating on their soles to move smoothly over unusual material. They are especially helpful when topstitching on oilcloth.

PRESSER FEET

"Super H" presser foot: This is often called an open-toe embroidery foot; it's commonly included with the purchase of sewing machines. I like to use this when I am attaching trim; it allows me to see exactly where I am sewing.

Teflon foot, Super H foot, roller foot

Pressing cloth: Usually white cotton, a pressing cloth is placed between the item being pressed and the iron for protection from the heat of the iron. These can be purchased or made at home; make sure the cloth you're using is large enough to cover your surface. See-through ones also are available.

Rotary cutter: One of the best inventions ever! A rotary cutter is a razor-sharp circular blade used to cut fabric precisely and quickly. Use a smaller cutter when cutting small curves and a larger cutter for straight lines. You can use them to cut several layers at once. Always cut upon a proper cutting mat and use your wide, gridded ruler to guide you.

Ruler: Essential for measuring, marking straight and perpendicular lines, and squaring corners on patterns and fabric. Get a wide, clear acrylic ruler meant to be used with a rotary cutter. Usually ⅛″ thick and gridded both horizontally and vertically, this will help you draw perpendicular lines for square corners. A useful size is 6½″ × 24″.

Seam gauge: A shorter ruler with an adjustable flange. Slide the flange up and down to check that seam allowances, hems, and hand stitches are even.

Seam ripper:
Necessary for pulling out stitches when you make a mistake. I use the 4-in-1 Essential Sewing Tool created by Alex Anderson. This super tool includes a seam ripper, stiletto, presser, and point turner.

Sewing machine: A regular sewing machine is all you need to use for all the projects in this book. A *serger* sewing machine can be handy, but it's not necessary. Just use pinking shears or a simple zigzag stitch to keep any seams from fraying.

Sewing machine needles: I stick with a universal needle in size 80/12. It's great for a wide range of fabrics, from linen to oilcloth. Remember to change your needle often for the best results.

Thread: I prefer a high-quality all-purpose thread for my sewing projects. Oilcloth does not require the use of heavy-duty thread.

Tracing wheel and tracing paper: A fast and effective pair of tools for transferring necessary marks from pattern to fabric. Put the colored, waxy side of the tracing paper against the wrong side of your fabric. Use a smooth-edge tracing wheel for oilcloth and laminated cotton, so as not to make holes in the material.

Water-soluble pen: An amazing tool for marking on the right side of fabrics, it's essential to mark topstitching lines and for many other uses. Wet the marks to make them disappear. It's best to test the pen on a scrap of fabric before using on a project.

tips and tricks

Bar tack: A bar tack is a handy stitch. To use it, drop the feed dogs and set your stitch to the widest zigzag. If you can't drop the feed dogs on your machine, set your stitch length to 0. It's great for attaching buttons and for securing seams.

Basting: A long stitch done by machine or by hand, used to hold layers of fabric or gathers in place. Stitch within the seam allowances.

Chain stitching: Sewing one seam and then another without clipping your threads. This saves time and materials. You get to fly through projects like a pro.

Clipping corners: Before turning a project right side out, cut straight across the tip of the corner, making sure not to snip too close to the stitching. Then cut diagonally toward the tip of the corner on both sides. Removing the extra fabric reduces bulk and ensures that your finished corners are sharp and pointed. The point turner on Alex Anderson's 4-in-1 Essential Sewing Tool is helpful for pushing out the corners after they are turned right side out.

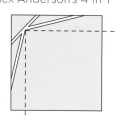

Crease-pressing:
When applying oilcloth trim to a project, since it can't be ironed, it's helpful to crease-press the trim first. Do so by folding the oilcloth trim in half and running the fold over the edge of a table. This will make a crease and act as a guide. If you have time, place the folded trim under a book for a few hours to set a sharp crease.

Cross-pinning:
Pinning pieces together by placing a pin in one direction and then another pin in the opposite direction so that the two pins make a cross. This really helps the seams stay put. I especially like to do this when pinning gathers or sharp curves.

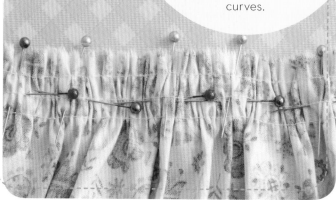

Edge stitch: When adding trim or under-stitching, edge stitching is a handy and professional skill to have. Using a Super H presser foot, move the needle position to the left. Line the left side of the trim up to the left inner side of the H and use the inside of the presser foot as a guide.

Embroidery and hand stitching basics: When you start a new strand of floss or perle cotton, knot an end so you don't accidentally pull the thread all the way through the fabric. From the wrong side, push your needle through the fabric where you won't be able to see it; I like to place this knot stitch so it will be hidden under another stitch. Just go through a few threads of the fabric and then go back to the wrong side of the fabric. Go back up and down through the same holes to knot off the thread. Refer to Hand Stitches (page 172) for the special hand stitches used in several projects.

Faux fancy foot: If you are just getting started and you don't have a fancy roller or Teflon presser foot, don't fret. Apply a bit of painter's tape or masking tape onto the bottom of your regular foot. Cover the sole of the foot with tape and then carefully trim off any tape that isn't touching the metal, using a craft knife.

Grain: *Your woven fabrics need to be on grain for all the projects in this book.* You know that your fabric is on grain when the lengthwise (warp) and crosswise (weft) threads of the fabric are at right angles. To find the crosswise grain, snip into the selvage and pull a thread so that the fabric puckers; cut the thread and pull it from selvage to selvage. Use this line as a guide for trimming the edge. Once you have a perfectly straight cut, fold the fabric in half lengthwise. If your cut edge does not match, the fabric is off grain. If it's just a bit off grain, you might be able to steam-press the fabric to rights. If the fabric is badly off grain, fold the fabric on the bias (a 45° angle to the straight grain) and pull carefully. Once the cut ends and selvages are perpendicular, it's officially on grain.

Handmade bias: When you can't find the perfect bias, you can always make your own. See Making Continuous Bias Strips, page 105.

Ironing laminated cotton: You can iron the back of laminated cotton with a high-temp iron by using a pressing cloth. Make sure that the fabric never touches the hot iron.

Ironing oilcloth: *Never* iron oilcloth in the traditional method. You can crease-press oilcloth by finger-pressing the material, running the fold over a table edge, or flattening folded oilcloth under a stack of books.

Notch or clip: Small clips cut into the seam allowance of a concave curve allow the fabric to expand and lie flat when it's turned right side out. Small notches cut into a convex curve take out the bulk. Both are great to make marks for lining up pattern pieces.

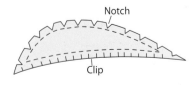

Notch

Clip

Pinning oilcloth: Straight pins can leave pinholes in oilcloth, so strategic pinning is a must. When laying out patterns, avoid pinning through the oilcloth on the inside of the pattern—the way we are used to pinning woven fabrics. Try pinning in the seam allowances or using pattern weights to secure your pattern while you trace it, and then you can cut.

Piping: Round trim stitched into seams or along edges in sewn projects. Refer to the Pillow Cover project (page 64) to make your own piping. It is fun and easy. Just start with bias and piping cord.

Slip stitch: A hemming stitch with the stitches on both the right and wrong sides of the fabric (see Hand Stitches, page 172). This stitch is great for closing up pillows, cushions, and hems.

Stitch in-the-ditch: Use your Super H foot and begin by dropping the sewing machine's needle between the two fabrics that meet at a seam. Stitch along the seamline, on the side without the seam allowances, while pulling the fabrics apart slightly on both sides of the seam as you sew. Sew slowly and steadily to avoid sewing outside the seamline. Using a stiletto can be helpful. There are also special stitch in-the-ditch feet with a center guide for perfect stitching.

Straight stitches: I am a bit picky with my stitches; I prefer to stick with a straight stitch. Over the years I've noticed that many people use a zigzag stitch when they make oilcloth goods, and while that's cute, I still find that the straight stitch looks more professional. So how do you sew a straight line? With practice, with patience, and by moving your needle around. I no longer use the seam gauge on my machine to keep me on track; now I line my project up to my presser foot and move my needle from side to side until I've got it where I need it. I won't kid you—topstitching on oilcloth can be a bear, so line it up and move slowly. Even if you're a seasoned pro at sewing with woven fabrics, I suggest that you use a scrap of oilcloth of equal thickness to practice until you get the hang of it.

Topstitching laminated cotton and oilcloth: Use a longer stitch length when topstitching on sticky fabrics such as laminated cotton and oilcloth. I like to use a length of 4. This will keep your fabric from getting caught up in the feed dogs. You'll be amazed that the stitches aren't too long.

bias tape

I just love bias tape; in fact, I never found a bias that I didn't love! Whether you're making your own or buying premade, bias is a very retro way to finish hems. It's great for adding a punch of color and vintage style to your projects. Bias is commonly found in single or double fold and in a variety of sizes.

Premade cotton bias: Many of the projects in this book suggest cotton bias tape; in some cases I suggest using the prepackaged variety, but only for practicality's sake! Please feel free to make your own bias for unique, one-of-a-kind projects.

Making cotton bias tape: See Making Continuous Bias Strips in the Trimmed Bed Skirt project, page 105.

Oilcloth bias tape: It isn't *technically* accurate to call this bias tape. Oilcloth isn't a woven material, so it has no weft, warp, or bias grain. When I refer to oilcloth bias tape, I mean that you simply cut 1"-wide strips of oilcloth and treat them as bias tape. Polka dots or oilcloth lace prints can be cut in crosswise strips to save yardage. If you're using a print like gingham, I suggest you cut it on the diagonal to get a diamond shape on your strips. Just use your clear gridded ruler to cut strips at a 45° angle. Oilcloth doesn't fray, so there is no need to fold the ends under; simply fold the fabric around the hem of the project and sew it in place.

Connecting cotton bias tape: It's easy to piece premade bias tape together once you've seen how to do it. Start by opening up the double-fold bias tape all the way and placing the two pieces right sides together so that they create a 90° angle. Pin and sew a diagonal line. Cut off

the extra, leaving a ¼" seam allowance, refold, and press.

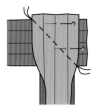

Connecting oilcloth bias tape: Because oilcloth does not fray, you can simply overlap the strips. To avoid pinholes in your trim/bias, pin the two together at a 45° angle to each other at the point where you want the stitch line to run. Sew a tight stitch from top to bottom. Clip your threads, and trim off the extra bit on either side of your seam.

Faux mitered corners: When applying bias tape or oilcloth trim to a project with corners, I suggest creating a faux mitered corner. Start by sandwiching the hem within the trim or bias tape, edgestitching in place all the way to the end of the corner, and backstitching. Remove from the machine and clip threads. Open up your folded trim and tuck the bottom half under the oilcloth. This creates a 45° angle at the corner. Now close the fold, encasing the project within the trim. Make sure your corners match up and create a tidy 45° angle. Pin and edgestitch. This works for both cotton and oilcloth bias tape.

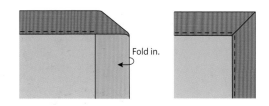

Fold in.

End fold finish for cotton bias tape: This is one of the simplest ways to finish off the ends of bias tape when hemming the bottom edge of a project (see Embellished Café Curtain, page 51). Start by adding a 1″ tail at each end of the tape. Pin the front fold of the bias to the fabric at each bottom corner. Open up the loose end of the bias tape, wrap the tail back to the wrong side of the fabric, and tuck it into the back fold of the trim. Pin and stitch in place at the corner, sew the rest of the bias, and then stop sewing when you are 4″ away from the end. Repeat to finish the other end.

Overlap fold finish for cotton bias tape: Start stitching at the very beginning of the cotton bias tape. Stop about 2″ away from where the two ends will meet. One edge is stitched down and the other has a loose tail, which should extend 1″ beyond the point where it meets the other end of your trim. Tuck under ½″ and let the additional ½″ overlap the stitched side of the bias. Pin and stitch to finish.

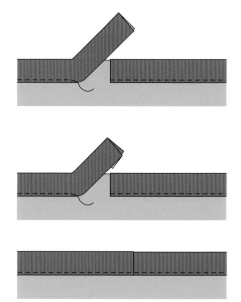

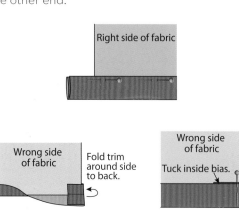

Right side of fabric

Wrong side of fabric

Fold trim around side to back.

Wrong side of fabric

Tuck inside bias.

Stitched finish for cotton bias tape:
This method of finishing bias tape creates a continuous loop and gives the project a pretty finish. Start by pinning the bias tape in place, leaving a few extra inches loose near the join. Make sure each end has an extra 2″. Bring both ends of the bias together so they are folded flush against each other. Iron to create a sewing guideline. Sew from top to bottom in the guideline and trim off all but ¼″ of bias. Press that seam allowance to one side. Refold the bias around the raw edge of your project and stitch it closed.

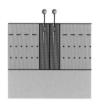

Finishing oilcloth bias: You can finish oilcloth bias just as you extended it. Cut it at an angle, and layer it on top of the oilcloth at the starting point. No need to fold the trim over. Pin on the top and from the back to ensure that you catch both sides of the oilcloth trim in one pass.

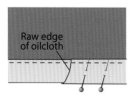

Raw edge of oilcloth

yardage calculation chart

Decimals	Yards	Inches
0.125	⅛	4½
0.167	⅙	6
0.25	¼	9
0.333	⅓	12
0.375	⅜	13½
0.5	½	18
0.625	⅝	22½
0.666	⅔	24
0.75	¾	27
0.875	⅞	31½
1	1	36

easy eyelet place mat

Finished size: 13½″ × 19″

No-sew projects make me happy. Couple that with one of my favorite fabrics and I am downright giddy! This chalk cloth place mat becomes a flexible and portable chalkboard for your dining room table. The place mats are great for parties or everyday meals with the family. You'll be making them for gifts for years to come.

Materials and Supplies

1 yard chalk cloth, 48" wide, for a set of 4

14" × 20" sheet of sturdy craft paper

Chalk

ADDITIONAL TOOLS

11/64" hole punch for leather

1/8" hole punch for leather

Hammer

preparing it

1. Photocopy the quarter place mat pattern (below), enlarging by 200%.

2. Cut out the enlarged pattern. Use the 11/64" hole punch to make holes on the 5 large circles along the scalloped edge of the pattern. Repeat with the 1/8" punch to do the remaining 10 small circles.

3. Fold the 14" × 20" sheet of craft paper in half vertically and horizontally; it's now in quarters. Open and draw lines along the 2 folds.

4. Place the copied pattern into the top right section of craft paper and trace.

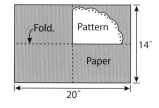

5. Fold the craft paper back into quarters so you can see the traced pattern on the outside; then cut out the scalloped edge.

6. Use the hole punch set to puncture all 4 layers of folded craft paper by tapping the butt of the punch with a hammer where indicated on the pattern.

7. Unfold your completed pattern.

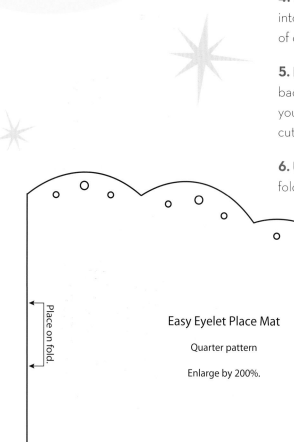

Place on fold.

Easy Eyelet Place Mat

Quarter pattern

Enlarge by 200%.

Place on fold.

cutting it out

1. Place chalk cloth on a smooth, flat surface, wrong side up. Place pattern according to the layout at right.

2. Trace each place mat using a fine-tip marker, marking the outer edge and each circle.

3. Using small snips or scissors, cut the place mat out. Avoid short, choppy cuts; instead, glide the scissors along each scallop.

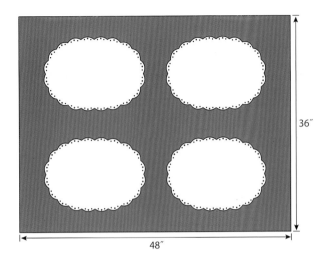

36"

48"

4. Lay a single place mat, wrong side up, on top of a scrap of wood or a self-healing cutting mat. Puncture a hole in each of the large circles using the ¹¹/₆₄" hole punch. Place the hole punch on the traced circle on the chalk cloth and tap the butt of the punch twice with the hammer. Then give the punch a twist clockwise to cut the threads on the back of the chalk cloth. Repeat with the ⅛" punch on the remaining small circles.

5. Trim any loose threads.

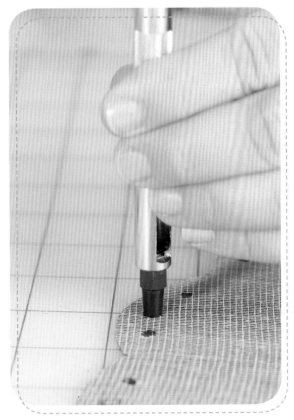

curing it

Chalk cloth needs to be cured or primed before use.

1. Lay a piece of chalk on its side on the chalk cloth surface, rub it all over from side to side, and then wipe clean with a damp cloth.

2. Do this another time, rubbing your chalk in the opposite direction.

3. Wipe it clean again, and the chalk cloth is now ready for use.

4. Grab some chalk and have a blast!

june suggests

Chalk cloth hates to be folded. Always keep your place mats rolled onto a cardboard pole to protect them from pesky creases.

Cured chalk cloth place mat

Photo by Nissa Brehmer

Grab some
chalk and start
doodling!

patchwork pot holder

Finished size: 8" × 8"

I am so drawn to feed sacks, with the soft touch of the worn fabric and the charming designs of the 1930s and 1940s. They are so homey. Large pieces of feed sack fabric can be costly, so when I found feed sack charm packs online, I was thrilled. A charm pack from your local quilt market or pretties from your own stash are sources for this project as well.

Materials and Supplies

1 feed sack charm pack or scraps from your stash

1 fat quarter of calico print for backing

⅓ yard of metalized Mylar insulated interfacing, 45" wide, such as Insul-Fleece by C&T Publishing

1 scrap of cotton batting, at least 10" × 10"

1 package of ½"-wide double-fold bias tape

☞ **TIP**

When using scraps, cut out your strips along the grain of the fabric. Pulling a loose thread to find the grainline will ensure that your project stays on the straight and narrow. (See *grain* under Tips and Tricks, page 15.)

preparing it

Photocopy or trace templates T and M onto template plastic or card stock and cut them out.

M
Cut 4.

Center

T
Cut 4.

Center

cutting it out

Charm Pack

1. Cut 36 strips 1½" × 5".

2. Cut 4 triangles using template T.

Calico

Cut 1 square 10" × 10".

Insulated Interfacing

Cut 1 square 10" × 10".

Batting

Cut 1 square 10" × 10".

constructing it

Block *All seam allowances are ¼″ unless otherwise noted.*

1. Lay out the 36 strips into 4 aesthetically appealing groups of 9.

2. Sew a group of 9 strips, long sides together, to create an outer unit. Repeat with the remaining 3 groups of strips.

3. Press all seams in the same direction. Mark the center of each outer unit through the long side with a pin.

4. Match up the center of template M with the center of each unit, and then trace and cut the units out.

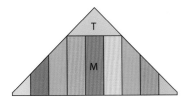

Mark and align centers.

5. Pin and stitch a triangle T to the top of each outer unit, right sides together, to create a quarter unit. Press seam toward outer unit.

6. Match the seams of 2 quarter units, pin, and stitch. Press to the side. Repeat with the last 2 quarter units, pressing the center seam in the opposite direction.

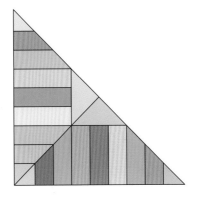

7. Pin the halves of the block together, matching the seams and nesting the center seam allowances, and sew them together. Press seams to the side.

8. Use a ruler to trim the quilt block down to an 8″ × 8″ square.

Pot Holder

1. Layer the calico 10″ × 10″ square, right side down, the insulated interfacing, the batting, and the completed block, right side up, centered on the lower layers. Pin or baste the layers together.

2. Quilt by *stitching in-the-ditch* (see Tips and Tricks, page 16).

3. Trim the batting and backing so they are even with the pieced block.

trimming it

1. Cut a piece of double-fold bias tape at least 37" long.

2. Start at a corner and sandwich the tape around only 1 side of the pot holder. Pin in place. Edgestitch along the first side. Remove the pot holder from the sewing machine, make a *faux mitered corner* (see Bias Tape, page 17), and continue to pin and stitch around the square, stopping 1" from the corner where you began.

3. Leave the last inch of the binding open but pin it in place around the pot holder. Stitch 5" of the loose end of the bias trim closed, and cut off any extra.

4. Twist the loose tail of bias into a loop on the back of the pot holder and tuck inside the binding that was left open in Step 3. Pin in place. Close up the loop by stitching the last bit of binding to the pot holder.

5. Fold the loop back onto the binding. Pin and stitch in place.

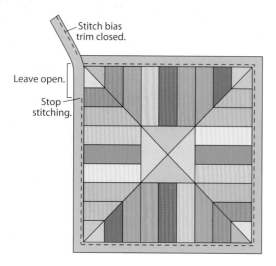

Stitch bias trim closed.

Leave open.

Stop stitching.

Now it's time to bake a yummy pie!

reversible floor mat

Finished size: 15″ × 24″

This reversible mat is perfect for use under pets' bowls or underfoot in the kitchen. Waterproof oilcloth mats are easy to clean—just wipe off with a damp cloth. Feel free to play with the size; make it bigger or smaller depending on your space and its intended use. Just make the smaller panel 3″ smaller than the desired overall size.

Materials and Supplies

1 yard of lattice oilcloth for the small front panel and the back panel

½ yard of floral or fruity oilcloth for the main front panel

⅔ yard of gingham oilcloth for bias trim

Double-stick tape

june suggests

Choose an allover print such as floral or lace oilcloth for the larger panel so you can see how pretty it is after you top it with the smaller piece.

cutting it out

1. From lattice oilcloth: Cut 1 rectangular panel 15″ × 24″ for the back and another panel 12″ × 21″ for the front.

2. From floral or fruity oilcloth: Cut 1 rectangular panel 15″ × 24″.

3. From gingham oilcloth: Refer to *oilcloth bias tape* (see Bias Tape, page 17) to cut enough strips 1″ wide on the true bias to yield 160″ in length.

making it

1. Refer to *connecting oilcloth bias tape* (see Bias Tape, page 17) to piece together all of the oilcloth bias strips into a single continuous piece.

2. Fold your 1″-wide bias strip in half lengthwise and finger-press it. (To finger-press oilcloth, press the fold between your thumb and forefinger to create a crease. It may take a few passes.)

3. Sandwich the trim around the outer edges of the 12″ × 21″ piece and pin in place, starting in the middle of a side. Pin parallel to where you will stitch to avoid pinholes in the mat. Edgestitch from the very beginning of the trim through all 3 layers, close to the raw edge of the trim. Refer to *faux mitered corners* (see Bias Tape, page 17) to make each corner.

☞ **TIP**

Be careful not to pull the trim too tight or your mat will not lie flat.

4. Stop stitching 2″ away from where the ends will meet. Cut the loose end of the trim on a slight diagonal ½″ beyond the beginning of the trim. Layer the loose tail over the beginning of the bias, pin, and stitch past your beginning stitches.

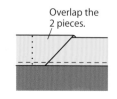

Overlap the 2 pieces.

5. Apply 1″ pieces of double-stick tape to the wrong side of the small panel at all 4 corners and in the center. Leaving a 1½″-wide border all around, center the small panel, right side up, on the top main panel, also right side up, using a wide acrylic ruler.

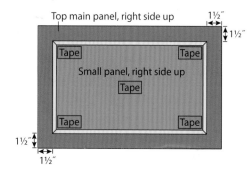

Top main panel, right side up   1½″

1½″

Tape   Tape

Small panel, right side up

Tape

Tape   Tape

1½″

1½″

6. Edgestitch ⅛″ away from the outside of the trim on the smaller panel, stitching it in place on top of the top main panel. Use your Super H presser foot (see *presser feet* under Tools, page 12) to guide the inner edge of the bias, and move your needle as needed for a nice straight line in just the right place.

7. Place the completed top main panel and back main panel *wrong* sides together. Pin them together around the outer edge of the mat.

8. Repeat Steps 3 and 4 to apply and edgestitch the remaining trim around the outer edge of the mat.

Photo by Nissa Brehmer

Your pet
never had
it so good!

grr's chicken scratch apron

Finished size: 34¼" × 20½"

My Grr (grandmother) was the only person I ever knew who wore an apron. I'll never forget her making oatmeal chocolate cookies with me while wearing an aqua gingham apron. That apron and those cookies instilled a desire to create a homey life filled with memories, and Modern June is a direct result of that desire.

Just one year into Modern June we lost Grr to a long and hard fight with Alzheimer's. The night of her wake I happened upon that aqua gingham apron in my aunt Peggy's garage, tucked in an open box. Years after Grr's death, my aunt Marianne sent me a handwritten copy of the pattern that Grr used to make the beloved apron and its "chicken scratch embroidery." The instructions are jumbled and lack the details a novice stitcher would need. But there in her own handwriting, I find inspiration! I've been saving this chicken scratch apron for something special. I hope it reminds you of someone equally as wonderful as my Grr.

Materials and Supplies

⅝ yard floral cotton fabric for apron body

⅝ yard polka dot fabric for waist-band and ties

¼ yard gingham fabric for accent

1 yard lightweight sew-in interfacing, 20" wide

4 yards of ½"-wide single-fold bias tape

2 skeins each of orange, white, and yellow embroidery floss (or colors that work with your fabrics)

june suggests

My grandmother used the following design to embroider aprons for Christmas gifts for many years. She always used black and white embroidery floss on a simple gingham fabric. I'm using fresh citrus colors for my modern approach to chicken scratch. I don't think she'd mind ... too much!

cutting it out

1. From floral: Cut 1 rectangular panel 18" × 34¼" for the apron body. Mark the center along 1 long side—this will be the top edge.

2. From polka dot: Cut 2 strips 7" × 29" for the apron ties and another strip 7" × 22" for the waistband. Cut 2 squares 7" × 7" for the pockets.

3. From gingham and interfacing: Cut 1 strip 5½" × 34¼" for embroidered contrast hem panel. Cut 2 rectangles 2¾" × 7" for the embroidered pocket trim.

embroidering it

To learn the stitches for this project, see Hand Stitches (page 172).

Contrast Hem Panel

1. Baste the 5½" × 34¼" gingham piece to the matching interfacing piece. You can skip this step if the apron print won't show through the gingham. However, if the apron fabric shows through, so will the reverse stitches.

2. Fold the gingham in half horizontally to find the centermost row with white squares. Lightly press with an iron to mark this important center line; it will serve a guide throughout the handwork process.

3. With a pin, mark a white square on the center line that is approximately 1½" away from the right-hand edge of the gingham.

4. Use a disappearing-ink marker to draw the pattern at right on the gingham, placing the rightmost snowflake in the design where the pin is.

- Draw the outer diamond of snowflakes on the white squares.

- Draw the inner snowflakes on the darker colored squares.

- Draw dashes on the lighter colored squares.

5. Place the marked section of the panel into a small embroidery hoop.

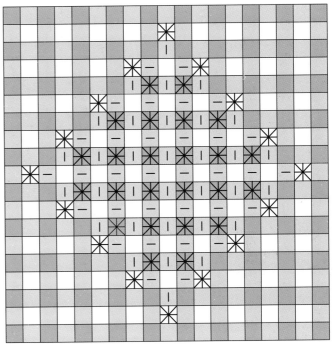

☞ **TIP**

Be careful not to stretch the fabric.

6. Embroider the design with 3 strands of embroidery floss, working counterclockwise. Work in a circle, being careful to stitch the same way each time.

- Snowflake stitch (page 173) the outer diamond in orange.

- Snowflake stitch inside the diamond in white.

- Use a running stitch (page 172) in white for the dashes.

- Use the woven circle stitch (page 173) in yellow to connect groups of 4 running stitches centered on a white square.

7. Skip a solid-colored square and repeat the diamond pattern 7 times, *moving from right to left.*

Chicken scratch diamond embroidery

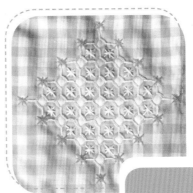

june suggests

Now that you have the hang of the stitches and the pattern, you might be able to skip marking all of the stitches. But if you get confused, slip off the embroidery hoop and draw the design again.

Pocket Accent

1. Baste the 2¾″ × 7″ gingham pocket trim and matching interfacing pieces together around the outer edges.

2. Use the stitch guide below to create a sweet little moment on the pocket trim. Center the design on your trim piece. My top 3 snowflakes were in white squares, but yours may be different. This pocket accent piece is so small that you don't need a hoop.

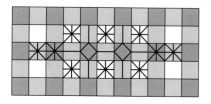

3. Stitch the snowflakes in orange, the running stitch in white, and the woven circles in yellow.

All seam allowances are ½″, unless otherwise noted.

1. Trim the top of the embroidered hem panel with bias tape. Pin and edgestitch in place, using your Super H foot to help stitch straight (see *presser feet* under Tools, page 12).

2. Pin the panel onto the bottom edge of your apron, aligning the raw edges at the bottom. Edgestitch the top edge of the panel directly onto your apron.

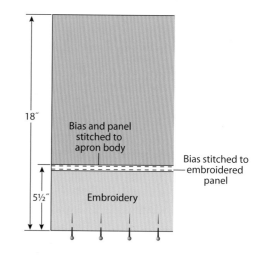

18″

5½″

Bias and panel
stitched to
apron body

Bias stitched to
embroidered
panel

Embroidery

3. Sandwich the bias tape around the sides and bottom of the apron and pin into place. Edgestitch, creating *faux mitered corners* (see Bias Tape, page 17) at the bottom. Set apron aside.

4. Trim the bottom edge of both embroidered pocket accent pieces with bias tape (it's the reverse of Step 1).

5. Align the raw edges of the trimmed accent pieces with the top of each pocket, pin, and edgestitch in place along the bottom of the bias.

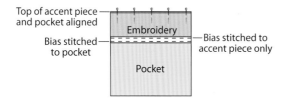

Top of accent piece and pocket aligned

Embroidery

Bias stitched to pocket — Bias stitched to accent piece only

Pocket

6. Pin and edgestitch bias tape to the top edges of the pockets, leaving a ½" tail on each end.

7. Place the pockets right side down on an ironing board and press ½" to the wrong side on the sides and the bottom. Tuck the extra bias trim inside the fold to create a clean pocket top. Use a clear ruler to make sure that your patch pocket is square. Reposition and re-press if not.

8. Pin each pocket to the apron 3" down from the top and 4" in from each side. Take care to tuck in the extra bias trim and the bulky folded corners; a few extra pins might be necessary. Edgestitch in place using a ⅛" seam allowance around the sides and bottoms. The top of your pocket is a high-stress area, so be sure to double-stitch the tops of the pockets on the sides. Do so by moving your needle over a click on the dial and repeating the stitching.

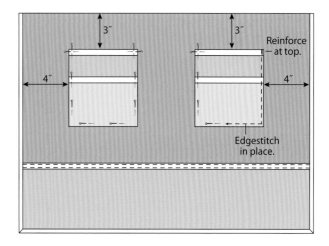

3"

3"

Reinforce at top.

4"

4"

Edgestitch in place.

9. Machine baste along the top edge of the apron twice—first ⅜" from the raw edge and then ¼" away from the first line—to create gathering threads.

10. Pin and sew the 7" × 29" ties to each short end of the 7" × 22" waistband piece, right sides together. Press your seams open.

11. Matching the centers, pin the waistband and apron body right sides together as shown. Align the sides of the apron body with the side seams in the waistband. Pull gently on the gathering threads and slide the fabric toward the center until the apron body is the same size as the waistband. Distribute gathers evenly and pin in place. Sew the 2 together using a ½" seam allowance. Remove the gathering stitches, and press the seams up and into the waistband.

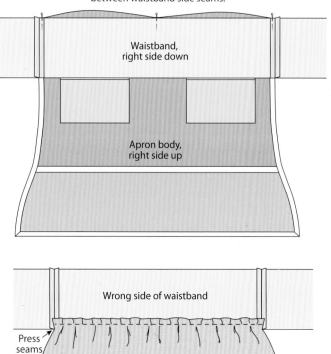

Gather apron body to fit
between waistband side seams.

Waistband,
right side down

Apron body,
right side up

Wrong side of waistband

Press
seams
up.

Wrong side of apron body

12. Fold the entire waistband in half lengthwise, right sides together. Starting at the side seams in the waistband, sew the ties closed along the bottom edges, creating a tube on each side of the apron. Draw a 45° angle at the end of each tie. Cut along this pencil line, pin, and sew shut. Turn ties right side out and press.

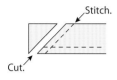

Stitch.

Cut.

june suggests

The ties are very long so that they can wrap around the back and tie in a bow at the front of your body. If you prefer to tie a bow in the back instead, you may wish to shorten the ties appropriately.

13. With the apron wrong side down on your ironing board, fold ½" of the back side of the waistband under, enclosing the seam allowances of the apron body and the waistband. Press and *cross-pin* (see Tips and Tricks, page 14) in place. Turn the apron right side up and edgestitch the apron's waistband closed.

Now it's time to whip up a batch of no-bake oatmeal chocolate cookies with someone special!

bar stool makeover

Finished seat size: 12½" diameter (customizable)

Plain Jane bar stools are easy to come by; buy them new, or better yet, find a set at a yard sale—or even pull them out of your own basement. Some foam and a bit of laminated cotton turns a ho-hum staple into a stellar and comfy focal point at the kitchen counter.

Materials and Supplies

½ yard each of 2 coordinating laminated cottons (for top of cushion and for piping)

⅛ yard of a coordinating laminated cotton for side of cushion

2½ yards of ³⁄₁₆"-diameter cable cord

18" × 18" square of 2"-thick foam

ADDITIONAL TOOLS

Staple gun and ¼" staples

Electric carving knife or serrated knife (*optional*)

 TIP

A can of top-quality spray paint goes a long way with this project. Pairing a glossy new finish with a bold print will help you create a one-of-a-kind look.

preparing it

Cushion Top

Use the seat of the bar stool to draw a circle on a piece of craft paper. Use a ruler or seam gauge to add a 1/2" seam allowance to your pattern all around; then cut the pattern out.

Welt

1. The side of a seat cushion is called the *welt*. To make the welt pattern, measure the depth of the wooden seat. Add this number to the thickness of your foam and then add 1" for seam allowances. Transfer these measurements to your craft paper.

Welt height example:
$^{3}/_{4}$" (seat) + 2" (foam) + 1" (seams) = $3^{3}/_{4}$"

2. For the length of the welt, multiply the seat's diameter by pi (π, 3.14) and add 1" for seam allowances.

Welt length example:
$12^{1}/_{2}$"(D) × 3.14 (π) + 1" (seams) = $40^{1}/_{4}$" length

3. Draw on craft paper and cut out a rectangle that is the height from Step 1 by the length from Step 2 for the welt pattern.

Piping

Since you will add piping to both sides of the welt, the finished length of piping is the length of the welt doubled. Add a few extra inches for joining. The width of the bias strips to cut is 1½".

Piping example:
$40^{1}/_{4}$" × 2 = $80^{1}/_{2}$"; round up to 86" of piping

cutting it out

1. From laminated cotton 1: Cut 1 cushion top using your pattern.

2. From laminated cotton 2: Cut 6 bias strips (page 17) 1½" wide for the piping and the seat bottom facing.

3. From laminated cotton 3: Cut 1 welt using your pattern.

4. From foam: Use your previously made cushion top pattern, *with the 1/2" seam allowance cut off,* to draw a circle onto the foam. Use an electric carving knife or serrated knife to cut the foam; place the foam on the edge of a sturdy work surface and go slow and steady. Pay extra attention to your safety. Keep the knife at a 90° angle so the cut sides of the cushion will be straight.

sewing it up

Use a ½" seam allowance unless otherwise stated.

Piping

Set aside 2 strips of 1½"-wide bias to use as the facing.

Refer to Making the Piping (Pillow Cover, page 66) to make piping using the cording and the 1½"-wide bias strips.

Welt

Pin and sew the short ends of the welt piece into a loop. Use a pressing cloth to press seams to the side.

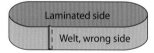

Seat Cushion Cover

1. Pin the piping onto the right side of the cushion top, aligning the raw edges. When you reach the beginning, cut the piping off, leaving a 1" tail loose. Use a seam ripper to open up the bias strip along the tail. Clip the piping's seam allowance to help it curve around the seat cushion cover.

2. Peel back the bias strip, exposing the end of the cording. Wrap tape around the loose end of the cording and cut it where it meets the beginning piping to make a perfect circle. Replace bias back over cording. Fold ½" of loose bias over to the wrong side and wrap it around the other end of the piping, overlapping and enclosing the piping.

Wrap folded end of bias over beginning.

3. Sew the piping onto the cushion top, stitching as close to the cording as possible. Repeat with the remaining piping on the bottom edge of the welt loop, starting and stopping at the seam.

4. Align the joins in the piping, pin, and stitch the unpiped edge of the welt to the piped seat cushion, right sides together.

5. Join together the 2 remaining 1½"-wide bias strips. Press the seam to the side, remembering to press on the wrong side of the laminated cotton using a pressing cloth. Starting at the welt seam, pin and sew the bias strip onto the bottom edge of the welt, right sides together, to create the bottom facing. Simply overlap the raw edges of the bias where they meet.

stapling it

1. Turn the sewn seat cushion right side out and insert foam.

2. Lay the seat cushion upside down on a work surface and set the seat of the stool on top of the foam.

3. Wrap the bias facing on the seat cushion cover to the underside of the wooden seat and staple into place. Do this in 4 places—at 3, 6, 9, and 12 o'clock—to evenly anchor the fabric in place.

4. Flip stool over and check the placement of your fabric. If you see any gaping or bunching of fabric, fix it now.

5. When the fabric is correctly situated onto the stool, flip it upside down again on the table and staple the remaining fabric in place.

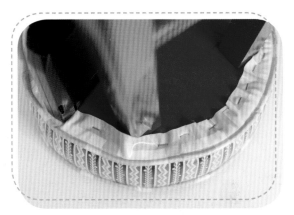

Now you'll be sitting pretty!

embellished café curtain

Finished panel: 24½" × 42" (customizable)

Café curtains have long been a staple in the kitchen, but this version is tricked out with vintage pot holders to add a little kitsch to the kitchen. It's best to install whatever of the many varieties of curtain hardware you choose prior to measuring and making the curtain.

Materials and Supplies

Lightweight linen/cotton blend fabric, 44" wide (or wider if needed)

46" double-fold bias tape *per panel**

46" rickrack *per panel**

Vintage pot holders, 2 per panel

Café curtain rod to fit your window, 1" diameter or smaller

* Measure your window's width and adjust accordingly.

june suggests

This is a basic café curtain pattern, so go wild with it and make it your own. Lengthen it to make sheers or create another casing and header at the bottom of a curtain to cover a set of French doors.

measuring it

1. Measure from the top of the rod to the windowsill; this is the height. Add 5″ to the height to determine the length of fabric needed for a single panel. My kitchen windows are 23″ high, so my fabric will need to be 28″ long.

2. For the width, measure from an inner edge of the window frame to the other inner edge—from side to side. Multiply this number by 1.5 to determine the width of the panel. My windows measure 29″, so my panel will be 44″—the width of my fabric. If you have wide windows, consider making 2 panels instead of seaming your fabric.

3. To determine the amount of fabric you need, take the measurement from Step 1 and multiply that by the number of curtain panels you need to make.

Example: For my project, 28″ × 4 = 3⅛ yards, so I purchased 3⅓ yards to cover any shortages.

4. Refer to *grain* (page 15, in Tips and Tricks) to cut the number of panels needed; pay attention to the grainline of the linen. A panel cut off grain will never hang right. Trim off the selvages and press any creases out of each panel.

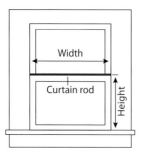

preparing it

After rounding up a good number of pot holders, soak them in a bath of oxygen-based detergent to remove any stains. Lay the pot holders flat and block them into shape by pinning. Allow them to air dry.

applying pot holders

1. Lay out a café curtain panel onto a worktable. Place the first pot holder 5″ away from the left side of the panel and 3″ from the bottom edge. Pin into place. Place the second pot holder 2″ to the right of the first. Next, draw a stitching line for the rickrack 2″ above the bottom edge of the panel with a water-soluble pen.

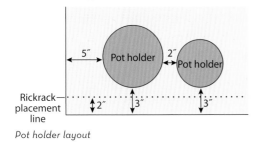

Pot holder layout

2. For pot holders that have pointed edges, it's best to *bar tack* (page 14, in Tips and Tricks) at the outermost edges. Switch to a wide zigzag stitch and drop your feed dogs so the machine doesn't pull the fabric. Stitch in place, creating a sturdy bar tack. Round pot holders can be sewn using a long basting stitch. You also can hand stitch pot holders in place.

3. Place ¼″ rickrack on top of the stitching line and stitch in place using a straight stitch and matching thread.

sewing it up

1. Turn the sides of the panel ¼″ toward the wrong side, press, turn an additional ¾″ to the wrong side, and press again. Pin and then edgestitch along the folds.

2. Along the top raw edge of the panel, turn under ½″ to the wrong side, press, turn under an additional 3″, and press again. Pin and edgestitch to make the casing.

3. Use a ruler and disappearing-ink marker to draw a stitching line 1½″ down from the top edge of the curtain. Stitch on the line to finish the casing and header; follow the manufacturer's instructions to remove the disappearing-ink line.

4. Refer to *end fold finish* (page 18, in Bias Tape) to hem the curtain with a piece of double-fold bias tape at least 2″ longer than the finished width of your panel.

Enjoy your cheery new café curtains!

bench redo

Finished size: varies depending on the bench used

Come see me do a presentation, and you'll see me do at least one stapling project. I love a good stapling project! The following process will work on dining room chairs, benches, and footstools alike. While shopping for furniture, look for pieces with detachable cushions—you know the type: they sit in every thrift shop covered in the ugliest fabric from decades past, just waiting for a second chance at life. When you've found the perfect chair, bench, and footstool, grab some fabric and your home tool kit, and create a unique conversation piece.

My choice for this project was made easy when my daughter and I spotted this set of nesting benches at a local antique store. The midcentury design lends itself to my decor and will give my small living room extra seating or tabletop space when needed. Between uses, I'll be able to stash it by one of our love seats, out of the way.

Materials and Supplies

Bench with detachable cushion panel

Laminated cotton, enough to cover the top and sides of bench plus 4″

Muslin, in an amount equal to laminated cotton

Replacement batting or foam (if needed)

ADDITIONAL TOOLS

Diagonal pliers

Screwdriver

Staple gun and ¼″ staples

4-in-1 Essential Sewing Tool (optional)

june suggests

This project is great for any number of fabrics. Oilcloth and laminated cotton are hard wearing, waterproof, and easy to clean, so they are my fabrics of choice. But pretty home decor fabric, burlap, or canvas fabrics work well, too.

preparing it

1. Most benches have a removable wooden board that serves as the cushioned panel for the bench; these are usually screwed in and detach easily. Remove the panel from the bench and set it aside. Store the screws in a safe place; you're going need them later.

2. Assess the condition of the bench. Does it need sprucing up? Now is the time to give it a good cleaning or a quick paint job.

3. Lay the wooden panel on a flat work surface, facedown. Use diagonal pliers to remove the staples that hold the old fabric in place. Diagonal pliers allow you to pry or dig out the staples more safely than a flathead screwdriver. Discard the old staples.

4. Take the fabric and whatever padding was originally used off the wood. Decide whether you have to replace the batting or foam. If it's compressed flat, the answer is yes, you do! Use the old material as a buying guide. Get the same style of batting or foam at the same size or larger. In my case the batting was too worn, stained, and smelly to be reused. I replaced it with 2 layers of dense batting.

5. Use the old fabric as a size guide for yardage. My 3 vintage benches used 3 squares of fabric 17" × 17", 19" × 19", and 21" × 21". These squares included extra material to cover the height of the batting and wood and to wrap under the bench. The 3 benches required just over 1 yard of 56"-wide laminate, but my fabric had a specific repeat to the print, so I bought 1½ yards of fabric. This allowed me to pick which part of the pattern I wanted to focus on.

cutting it out

1. Lay the new batting or foam facedown onto a flat worktable.

2. Using the wood panel as a template, trace it onto the foam or batting with a permanent marker. Cut it out. If you're using batting, use a good pair of scissors. For foam, use a large serrated knife.

3. Use the wood as a pattern again, this time for the laminate. Move the wood piece around until you have centered it onto the part of material you like best—make sure you have a few extra inches on all sides. Carefully flip the laminate and the wood over to make sure you like what you see. When you have the wood in the right spot, turn it and the laminate over again facedown on the table.

4. Lightly trace the shape of the board onto the laminate with a pencil—you don't want to see ink marks on the right side of the material.

5. Layer the batting or foam onto the wood and measure their combined height. In my case, the wood was ⅜" thick and the batting an extra ¼", so together they came to ⅝". Add 1" to this measurement and write this number down.

6. Go back to your laminated cotton, which is still on the table upside down. With a ruler, draw a border around the penciled pattern that is the same amount larger as the number you wrote down in Step 5. This border is the fabric that will cover the side of the cushion unit and the bottom perimeter of the wood—in other words, the up-and-under bit. Cut away extra fabric.

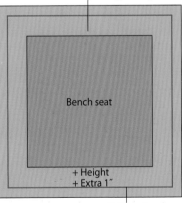

Cotton laminate, wrong side up

Bench seat

+ Height
+ Extra 1"

Cutting line

stapling it

1. Center the batting onto the wrong side of the laminate. Now layer your wood on the batting, taking care to match up the edges with the penciled square.

2. Using the staple gun, attach the center of the fabric to the center of the wood on any side. Pivot the cushion unit 180°, and pull the fabric on the opposite side of your first staple so that it is taut but not tight; then staple it into the wood.

Staple opposite sides.

☞ **TIP**

When possible, rest the staple gun on the wooden surface. This will help the staples to go in flush. If they aren't flush, the staple is too long. I find that a ¼" staple is best for most projects.

3. Repeat by stapling the center of the next 2 sides. Then, pivot until you have 2 or 3 staples holding the fabric on all sides. Again, pull evenly so that your finished product is evenly secured. Mark the screw holes with a pencil mark.

Mark screw holes.

4. Flip your cushion and make sure that it looks nice. If you have any indentations or stress points, remove the staples and redo them. This is the beauty of a staple project; it's fast, and it's easy to fix trouble spots.

5. Now it's time to work on the corners. Start by folding over a corner of the laminate so that it makes a 90° angle opposite the corner of the board. Staple in place near the edge of the wood. Repeat on the next 3 corners. Trim off the tip of each corner.

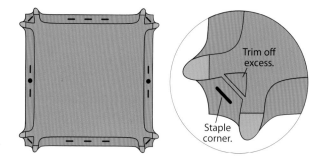

Trim off excess.

Staple corner.

6. Working from the center to the corners, finish stapling the sides.

7. Finish by folding up the corners. Tuck the loose fabric in so that it creates a 45° angle and a tiny pleat on the side of the cushion. Then staple it in place. Repeat this process twice on each corner.

june suggests

For a professional touch use an extra piece of fabric to cover the bottom of the wood. Cut a piece of coordinating fabric of any type ½˝ smaller than the cushion. Staple it in the center of each side and on the corners.

8. Use the stiletto on the 4-in-1 Essential Sewing Tool (or another sharp, pointed object) to poke holes in the laminate where you marked the screw holes. Then screw the cushion back onto the bench.

Sit back, put your feet up, and dream about your next easy stapling project.

panel drapes

Finished size: 50" × customized length each

Make 2 panels per window.

Dressing up a window with flat panel drapes helps add a bit of finish to a home. The huge variety of fabrics now available means that you are no longer forced to use traditional prints. Shopping online is a great way to find cool fabric to fit your style. Most companies offer swatches to help you choose the right color and print.

Materials and Supplies

Home decor fabric, 56" wide

Drapery lining, 56" wide

4"-wide fusible buckram header tape

7 drapery rings per panel to fit your curtain rod

7 long-neck drapery hooks per panel

1 curtain rod with brackets per window

2 drapery weights per panel

measuring it

1. Hang your desired curtain rod. Positioning the rod 4" above the widow trim is common. Extending the rod 2"–6" wider than the widow trim allows the panels to stack neatly out of the way and let in more light.

2. I used a full panel of 56"-wide drapery fabric, so the added fullness is already factored into this pattern. If you have narrow windows, you might opt to cut down the width of your panel, as a drapery panel is typically 1½ to 2 times wider than the window.

3. Measure the length from the top of the rod to the bottom of the windowsill or to the floor—whichever length suits the room best. Subtract the diameter of the curtain rings. This is the finished length for the drapery panel.

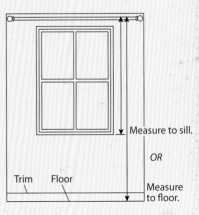

Measure to sill.

OR

Measure to floor.

Trim   Floor

cutting it out

Drapery Fabric

1. To determine the cut length, add 13" to the finished length.

2. Trim the selvage edges off the fabric and cut a panel that is the width of your fabric × the cut length.

Lining Fabric

1. To determine the lining cut length, subtract 3" from the drapery cut length.

2. The cut width of your lining fabric will be 6" narrower than the width of your drapery fabric.

3. Making sure to trim *both* selvage edges off the lining fabric, cut a panel according to the lining cut width × lining cut length.

sewing it up

Hemming the Panel

1. Your 2 drapery panels need to be hemmed a total of 5" at the bottom. Do this by turning 2½" along the bottom raw edge of each panel to the wrong side and press; then turn up a second 2½" and pressing once more. Pin at the sides of the panel first so your hem isn't askew; add several pins throughout the hemline. Use your sewing machine to sew the hem if you don't mind a visible stitch line. Or if you prefer a more refined finish, slipstitch (page 172) the hem closed by hand. My home is casual enough that I opted for a machine hem.

2. The lining panels need to be hemmed 2" total. Repeat Step 1, but turn only 1" to the wrong side each time. Definitely machine hem the lining!

Making the Panel

1. Align the top edges of a drapery panel and a lining panel, right sides together, and pin together along the sides. *Note: There will be extra drapery fabric in the center at this point.* Sew them together using a ½" seam allowance, creating a long tube, sewing from top to bottom on each side to avoid stretching out the fabric. Repeat this step with the second set of panels.

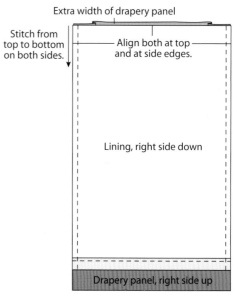

Extra width of drapery panel

Stitch from top to bottom on both sides.

Align both at top and at side edges.

Lining, right side down

Drapery panel, right side up

2. Turn both sets of lined drapery panels right side out. Lay the panel, lining side up, on a large, clean surface. Smooth out the drapery fabric underneath and center the lining so that an even 1½" of the drapery fabric shows along the sides of the lining. Pin the lining in place, so that it doesn't shift, and neatly press the side seams and outermost edges of the panel.

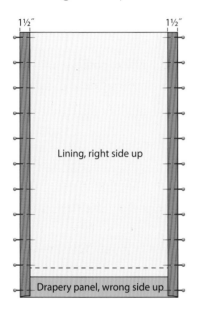

1½"   1½"

Lining, right side up

Drapery panel, wrong side up

Finishing the Hem

Fold the bottom and side edges of the drapery panels into 2 mitered corners where they meet. Place a drapery weight into each corner and stitch the fold closed by hand using a slip stitch.

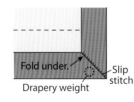

Fold under.

Slip stitch

Drapery weight

Creating the Header

1. Cut a piece of 4"-wide fusible buckram to the finished width of your panel. At the top of the lined drapery panel, pin and press the cut piece of buckram into place. Turn the header over once to the lining side, and then again, encasing the buckram.

2. Edgestitch the header closed using your machine's Super H foot (see *presser feet* in Tools, page 12). Slipstitch the openings closed on each end.

hanging it up

1. Across the top of your panel you'll be threading hooks right into the header. Starting in the center, place a hook ½" from the top edge. Add 2 hooks that are 1" in from the side hems. Now space the remaining 4 hooks an equal distance apart. On a 50"-wide finished panel, the hooks will be 8" apart.

2. Slide each hook into the smaller eyelet ring on the drapery rings.

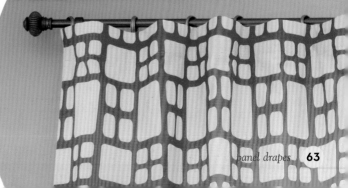

Doesn't that make a wonderful addition to your room?

pillow cover

Finished size: 16" × 16" to 24" × 24"

Pillows can be your best friends in home decor. A few new pillow covers can freshen up a room in no time. All you need is a bit of fabric, a few notions, and a pillow form—and you're set.

Materials and Supplies

½ to ¾ yard midweight home decor fabric, 54″ wide (depending on pillow size)

⅝ yard contrasting midweight home decor fabric for bias

2–3 yards ½″-diameter cording (depending on pillow size)

Invisible zipper 1″ smaller than pillow form

Square pillow form

june suggests

Oilcloth is a great fabric to use outdoors. Just skip the piping and you'll have a pretty set of weather-friendly pillows.

cutting it out

Pillow Fabric

1. Cut 2 squares of fabric that are 1″ larger than the pillow form (that is, for a 16″ × 16″ pillow, cut 2 squares 17″ × 17″).

2. At the bottom edge of both squares cut in Step 1, measure 2″ from each corner and make a small mark within the ½″ seam allowance as shown. Make another mark at the center. These marks are for zipper placement.

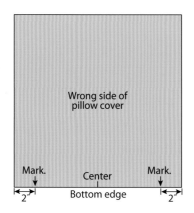

Piping Fabric

To figure out how much piping you'll need for a single pillow, multiply the width of your pillow by 4 and add an extra 4″.

Example:
16″ × 4 = 64″ + 4″ = 68″ piping

Refer to Making Continuous Bias Strips in the Trimmed Bed Skirt project (page 105) to make a continuous bias strip 2½″ wide. A 20″ × 20″ square of fabric will produce enough bias for a pillow up to 24″ × 24″.

sewing it up

Making the Piping

1. Lay the cording in the center of the continuous bias strip, wrong side up, and fold the fabric over it, keeping the cording in the center and aligning the raw edges of the bias strip. Pin to hold in place.

2. Leave the first 2″ of the continuous bias strip unstitched. Using a zipper foot, sew the bias strip closed so the cording is tightly enclosed. I don't use the seam gauge on the machine as my sewing guide on this step; instead, I concentrate on snugging up to the cord. Your seam allowance will end up around ½″ for nice, pretty piping.

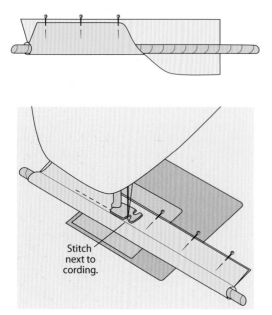

Stitch next to cording.

Attaching the Piping

1. Fold 1″ of the loose bias strip on the piping to the inside, and finger-press a quick crease. Pin the piping around the outer edge of the front pillow square, right sides together, aligning the raw edges.

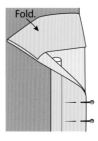

Fold.

2. Clip into the piping's seam allowance to allow for movement as you pin at the corners.

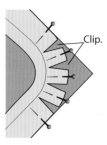

Clip.

3. When you near the starting point, refer to Seat Cover Cushion in the Bar Stool Makeover project (pages 47 and 48) to trim the ends of the cording flush with each other and close up the piping.

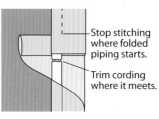

Stop stitching where folded piping starts.

Trim cording where it meets.

Installing the Zipper

1. Open the zipper and press the tapes flat. This will remove the zipper's curl and you'll be able to get the needle in closer without a fancy invisible zipper foot. The regular zipper foot will be just fine now.

2. Position the top of the zipper at the 2″ mark along the bottom of the pillow front. Open up the zipper and pin it next to the piping, right sides together. Sew as close as you can to the piping, closing the zipper as you reach the end so that you can stitch all the way down.

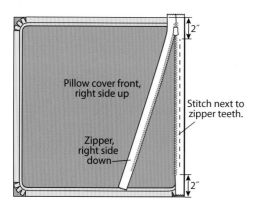

Pillow cover front, right side up

Stitch next to zipper teeth.

Zipper, right side down

2″

2″

3. Close the zipper completely and with a pencil draw a light line across your zipper seam allowances at the 2″ and the center marks. Use these lines to match up the zipper perfectly to the other pillow square. Pin the zipper to the pillow square, right sides together.

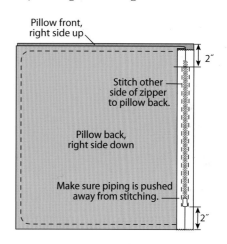

Pillow front, right side up

2″

Stitch other side of zipper to pillow back.

Pillow back, right side down

Make sure piping is pushed away from stitching.

2″

4. Sew the other side of the zipper as close to the coils as possible. Move the zipper pull up and down as needed to stitch the entire length of the zipper.

Making the Pillow

Important: Open the zipper halfway so you can turn the pillow right side out later!

1. With the piped side up, pin the 3 open sides of the pillow right sides together, matching the corners and edges.

2. Starting ¼″ inside from the zipper, sew the pillow cover together, stitching on top of the previous stitching line for the piping. Avoid the coils of the zipper at the bottom corners. At the end, sew ¼″ beyond where the zipper stop would be if the zipper were closed. Doing so closes up the zipper opening and makes for a nice finished product.

3. Clip the corners of the pillow front and back. Turn your pillow right side out and fill it with a pillow form.

Amazing how a few new pillows spruce up a room!

umbrella-ready tablecloth

Finished size: 54″ × 76″ (customizable),
to fit a 1½″- to 1¾″-diameter umbrella pole

We've all been there at one time or another. You want to set the patio table with a nice tablecloth and dine alfresco, but that pesky umbrella pole is in the way. This low-maintenance tablecloth is made with hard-wearing oilcloth and is tricked out with hook-and-loop tape so you can close it around the umbrella pole. Oilcloth is waterproof and doesn't stain easily.

Materials and Supplies

(Yardage depends on table size.)

Oilcloth

1″-wide hook-and-loop tape

½″-wide purchased double-fold bias tape

june suggests

Another great fabric for this type of tablecloth is outdoor fabric. Look for waterproof fabric with a UV protectant. Oilcloth isn't treated for fading, so avoid long exposures to full sun.

measuring it

1. Measure the width and length of your patio table. Add 16" to both of these measurements to allow for an 8" drop on all 4 sides of the table.

My table is 38˝ × 60˝, so my finished tablecloth is 54˝ × 76˝.

2. To determine the amount of fabric you need, take the length measurement from Step 1, multiply by 2, and then divide by 36 to get the yardage needed.

My yardage:
76˝ (the finished length) × 2 = 152˝ ÷ 36 = 4¼ yards

3. Most oilcloth comes in bold prints, so be sure to buy more than you need to match up your prints. A print will have a repeat. A fabric vendor can help you figure out the size of the repeat.

My material has a 9˝ repeat to the print, so I needed an extra ½ yard to match the print. I simply added the ½ yard to my 4¼ yards, so I bought 4¾ yards.

4. Your tablecloth will have a seam running along the length—on 1 side of the umbrella it will be sewn shut, and the other side can be opened and closed via hook-and-loop tape. The length of the hook-and-loop tape needs to be half of the finished length of the tablecloth.

Example:
76˝ ÷ 2 = 38˝, so I bought 1⅛ yards

5. To determine how much binding you need, add the finished length to the finished width and double it. Add a few extra inches for seams.

Example: Finished tablecloth is 54˝ × 76˝;
54˝ + 76˝ = 130˝ × 2 = 260˝, or 7¼ yards

cutting it out

1. Copy and cut out the pattern on page 73 onto sturdy paper.

2. Cut 1 piece of oilcloth to the finished length × width of the material. Mark the midpoint along a long edge with a pin.

3. Using the pinned midpoint, match the pattern at the pinned edge to the remaining longer piece of oilcloth. Mexican oilcloth is pretty busy, so matching it up perfectly is not always possible. When you are happy with the placement, use another pin to mark the center of the second piece.

4. Trim the longer piece from both edges to the finished length of your tablecloth.

5. Fold a tablecloth panel in half at the center pin, right sides together, through the width of the material. With the center pin at the side closest to you, draw a line 1″ away from the selvage edge closest to you to mark the hook-and-loop tape placement. At the center pin, use your pattern to draw what looks like half of an archway, as shown, on the tablecloth panel, for the umbrella opening.

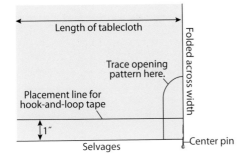

6. Flip the folded panel over and draw a line from the center pin 1½″ in from the selvage edge, running the length of the panel, to mark the cutting line for the closed end of the tablecloth.

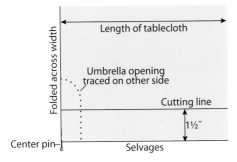

7. Repeat Steps 5 and 6 with the other cut panel so that the halves of the tablecloth are mirror images.

8. To determine how much excess width you need to cut from the long sides of the tablecloth, first divide the finished width in half, and then add ½″ for the seam allowance.

The width of my finished tablecloth needed to be 54″, so I divided 54″ by 2, added ½″, and came up with 27½″.

Keep the fabric folded, measure that distance across the panel from the 1½″ cutting line, and cut any excess width from the opposite side through both layers. Any extra can be used to make pillows for the deck!

9. Making sure that you've positioned the openings correctly as shown, use a pair of small snips to carefully cut the umbrella opening—take your time cutting out the curve. It will become the hole for the umbrella pole, and you don't want it to get too large.

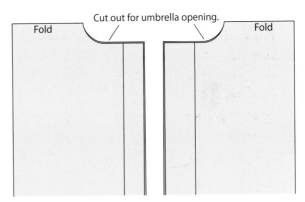

10. Unfold each piece and cut along the 1½″ line from Step 6.

Now you're ready to sew it up!

sewing it up

1. Using a ½" seam allowance, sew the panels right sides together along the side trimmed in Cutting It Out, Step 10. Fold the seam allowance to the side. Using a Super H foot and ⅛" seam allowance, topstitch the seam flat through all 3 layers.

2. Lay the tablecloth faceup on the work surface. The open sides of the tablecloth will naturally fold over each other. Use the 1" line drawn in Cutting It Out, Step 5 (page 71), to fold both edges over toward the right side of the oilcloth to create a stitching guide for the hook-and-loop tape.

3. Make sure that the right-hand panel is overlapping the left. On the overlapping panel, align the loop side of the tape to the right of the stitching guideline (the 1" fold line from the previous step). Place a single pin at the top of the tape. Pinning into hook-and-loop tape is hard enough; add oilcloth to that, and it's really hard on your hands. So use only a single pin; it will be plenty to keep you on track.

4. Stitch the hook tape in place along the *right-hand edge only*—this is another great time to use that Super H foot.

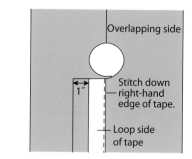

Overlapping side

1"

Stitch down right-hand edge of tape.

Loop side of tape

5. Fold the oilcloth back to the wrong side at the stitched side of the tape, flip the tablecloth over, and stitch the opposite edge of the tape through both layers of oilcloth.

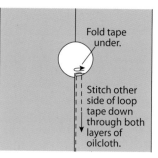

Fold tape under.

Stitch other side of loop tape down through both layers of oilcloth.

6. On the left-hand panel of the tablecloth, place the hook side of the tape to the *left* of the stitching guideline (the 1" fold line from Step 2), pin, and edgestitch in place along both sides.

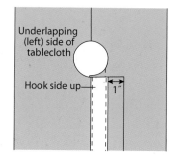

Underlapping (left) side of tablecloth

Hook side up

1"

 *edging it*

Refer to *connecting cotton bias tape* (page 17, in Bias Tape) if you need to join the double-fold bias tape to get the length needed. Starting in the middle of a side of the tablecloth, sandwich the edges within the bias tape, leaving a 5″ tail of bias unsewn at the beginning, and then edgestitch it into place. Refer to either method to finish the cotton bias tape (page 18, in Bias Tape) to connect the ends of the bias trim.

Care Instructions

Oilcloth is amazing. Just wipe it down, and you're ready for your next meal.

It can weather the rain, but the sun can do a number on your pretty tablecloth. To avoid deep creases when you store your oilcloth tablecloth, keep it rolled instead of folded between uses.

Umbrella
opening
pattern

Fire up the grill; it's almost dinnertime!

repurposed bunting

Finished size: 2 buntings, each 94″ long with 9 flags

Buntings are all the rage; you can't have a party without one. Make this pretty bunting trimmed in rickrack using vintage sheets, like mine, or use the quilting cotton of your choosing. Hunt for vintage sheets at your favorite thrift shop or buy them on etsy.com.

Materials and Supplies

3 coordinating fat quarters (18″ × 21″) vintage sheet material (approximately 3 pillowcases) for flags

3 fat quarters or 1 yard quilting cotton for back side of flags

1¾ yards of lightweight fusible interfacing, 20″ wide

2 packages premade ½″-wide double-fold bias tape (or at least 5½ yards)

3 packages baby rickrack, ¼″ wide (or at least 10½ yards)

preparing it

Pattern

Copy or trace the flag pattern (page 76) onto card stock and cut it out. Fold your pattern in half lengthwise to make sure it is symmetrical. Start over if not.

Fabric

Following the manufacturer's instructions, iron the interfacing to the wrong side of the 3 fat quarters of sheeting to give it a firmer hand. I recommend using a pressing cloth.

1. Trace the flag pattern as shown 6 times onto the right side of the interfaced fat quarter of sheeting. Repeat with the remaining 2 fat quarters. *Do not cut the pieces out yet.*

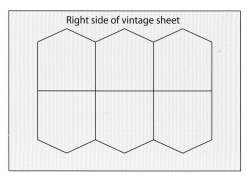

Right side of vintage sheet

2. Use a clear, wide ruler (such as a rotary-cutting ruler) and a disappearing-ink pen to draw 3 lines on the flag pieces. The first line starts 2″ in from the point of each bunting piece; draw the second and third lines each ½″ further away from the point. Because you haven't cut the flags out yet, you can draw a line across 3 pieces at a time. Repeat this step to mark the remaining 2 fat quarters.

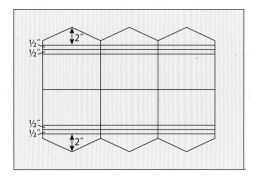

Repurposed Bunting
flag pattern

Cut 18 of vintage sheet fat quarters.
Cut 18 of quilting cotton.

trimming it up

1. Use the Super H presser foot (see *presser feet* on page 12, in Tools) on your sewing machine, and set your stitch length a bit shorter than normal, so your stitches won't pull out at the edges. With the presser foot in the up position, place a sheeting fat quarter, right side up, so that the stitching line closest to the point is centered under the foot. Place the baby rickrack on top of the first flag on the stitching line. Following the line, slowly and carefully sew through the center of the rickrack all the way across the fat quarter, stitching over all 3 flags in the row at once.

2. When you get to the end of the line, line up a second fat quarter under the rickrack and *chain stitch* (page 14, in Tips and Tricks). Repeat with the third fat quarter and trim the rickrack at the end of the fat quarter.

3. Repeat Steps 1 and 2 until you have all 3 rickrack lines stitched on all 18 flag fronts (6 rows of rickrack on each fat quarter).

cutting it out

1. Lay out each of the fat quarters, right side up, on top of the quilting cotton, wrong side up; pin them together and cut the flags out through both layers of fabric, using scissors or a rotary cutter and mat. As you cut the flags apart, you will also cut the rickrack. *Note: It may be easier to cut the quilting cotton into fat quarters before pinning.*

2. Cut 2 pieces of purchased double-fold bias tape each 95" long.

sewing it up

1. Separate the flag fronts (sheeting) and flag backs (quilting cotton) into 2 separate piles. Press each trimmed flag front from the wrong side.

2. Pin each flag front to a flag back, right sides together; then sew them together along the sides and bottom only, using a 1/4" seam allowance. Leave the top open for turning.

3. Clip the corners and points; then turn each flag right side out. Use a point turner or a chopstick to make sure that the corners and points are nice and neat. Press each flag flat, working from the back or with a pressing cloth.

4. Baste the top of each flag closed.

5. Open up an end of the 95"-long piece of bias tape. Fold 1/2" of this end in toward the wrong side, refold, and pin closed. Repeat on the other end.

6. Place a pin 18" from each end of the bias tape. (This pin indicates where the bunting pieces start and end, thus creating 2 ties of 18" for the finished bunting.) Insert 9 completed flags inside the fold of the bias tape, between the pins, spacing them an equal distance apart. Pin in place.

7. With the Super H foot, edgestitch the bias tape closed from end to end, using a 1/8" seam allowance, securing the flags in place.

8. Repeat Steps 5–7 to assemble the second bunting.

Now it's party time!

potting bench cover-up

Finished size: customizable

A potting bench is a handy piece of outdoor furniture to have around. Its job is to store pots, tools, and soil and to provide a place to do the dirty work. Because we don't always want to see what's underneath, I've created this cover to hide all the bags of whatnot. Hook-and-loop tape makes this pretty oilcloth curtain removable, so it's easy to get to your potting supplies. And the waterproof oilcloth helps keep the weather from rusting your tools and turning your dirt to mud.

Materials and Supplies

Yardage of polka dot oilcloth for panels (amount varies depending on size of bench)

½ yard gingham oilcloth for trim

Fat quarter fruit or floral oilcloth

1"-wide hook-and-loop tape (amount varies depending on size of bench)

Double-stick tape

ADDITIONAL TOOLS

Staple gun and ¼" staples

june suggests

This pattern can be used in several other ways with a bit of modification. For a cheap and easy bathroom make-over, just flip the hook-and-loop tape to the other side and make the cover-up wide enough to wrap around an out-dated bathroom vanity.

measuring it

1. Measure the width and length of the openings that you wish to cover on your potting bench. I chose to cover all 4 openings: the front, back, and both sides.

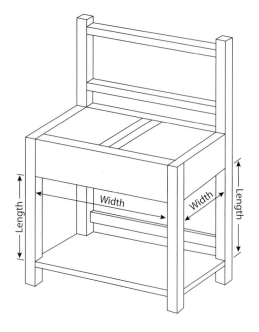

2. To calculate the amount of material needed, add 1" to the length for each opening. Follow the examples below depending on the width of your panels to determine the yardage you need to purchase.

If your openings are wider than 23½" but narrower than 47", you can cut a single piece across the width of your oilcloth. Openings that are narrower than 23½" (half the width of the oilcloth) can be cut 2 across the width of your oilcloth.

Example:
To cover 4 sections that are each 21½″ long but wider than half the width of the oilcloth:

21½″ + 1″ seam allowance = 22½″ × 4 panels = 90″; 90″ ÷ 36″ = 2½ yards

To cover 4 sections, each 21½″ long, but with 2 side panels that are narrower than half the width of the oilcloth:

21½″ + 1″ seam allowance = 22½″ × 3 = 67½″÷ 36″ = 1⅞ yards

I often buy a little extra, just in case.

cutting it out

1. From polka dot oilcloth: On the back of the material, draw—with a pencil—the width and length of the opening. Then add 1″ to the length for the hook-and-loop header. This will be the top of your panel curtain. You do not need to add any seam allowance or hems for the panel. Repeat this for every opening that you will cover.

2. From gingham oilcloth: To determine how much bias trim you will need to cut, multiply the width of each panel × number of panels. Multiply the length of each panel × 2 × number of panels. Add these subtotals together. Divide by 25″ (the length of a strip cut from 18″ of oilcloth at a 45° angle) to determine the number of strips to cut.

> *Example:*
> *44″ (width) × 2 panels = 88″*
>
> *20″ (width) × 2 panels = 40″*
>
> *22½″ (length) × 2 × 4 panels = 180″*
>
> *88″ + 40″ + 180″ = 308″ ÷ 25″ = 12.3,*
> *rounded up to 13 strips*

Cut enough 1″-wide strips at a 45° angle to trim both sides and the bottom of each panel.

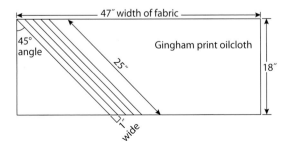

3. From fruit or floral oilcloth: Cut a series of flowers or a bunch of fruit from the oilcloth fat quarter to appliqué to your curtain panel(s). Use as many or as few motifs as you like.

4. From hook-and-loop tape: Cut 4 pieces of the *hook side only* of the hook-and-loop tape to match the width measurements of your bench.

sewing it up

1. Refer to Bias Tape (page 17) to connect the bias strips, making sure to match the gingham patterns.

2. Refer to *crease-pressing* (page 14, in Tips and Tricks) to press the joined 1″ strip in half lengthwise. Sandwich the trim around the panel, starting at the top right-hand corner. Pin and edgestitch the trim in place with a ⅛″ seam allowance, using the Super H foot, making sure to keep the pins along the ⅛″ seamline. Refer to *faux mitered corners* (page 17, in Bias Tape) to miter each corner.

3. Along the top edge of each panel on its right side, stitch the soft side of the hook-and-loop tape ⅛″ away from the top edge. Use the Super H foot and move the needle to the right to get as close to the edge of the tape as possible.

4. Sew the left edge of the loop tape in place; make sure to move the needle to the left this time. Carefully trim off any extra loop tape at the ends.

5. Place your oilcloth fruit or flower appliqué as desired on the panel(s) and adhere it with double-stick tape. Stitch around the outline of the appliqués, ⅛″ from the edge.

6. Staple the cut pieces of the hook side of the hook-and-loop tape to the underside of your potting bench. Press each panel into position.

Now it's time to pot some plants. Don't worry about getting your cute curtain dirty; just pull the panels off and hose it down when you're done.

BED AND BATH

color block duvet cover

Finished size: Twin, 69" × 87"

No one can debate the practical attributes of a good duvet cover; it's so easy to take care of. And let's face it—kids are messy creatures, so this is a perfect project for a child's or teenager's room. The following duvet cover is for a standard twin-size bed and can be used in a boy's or girl's room. In this age of high-quality quilt fabric, the possibilities are endless.

Materials and Supplies

½ yard each of 4 different fabrics for rectangles C, D, E, and G

1 yard each of 3 different fabrics for rectangles A and H and square B

1¼ yards of fabric for square F

2½ yards each of 2 different fabrics for the backing

Purchased twin-size comforter

36″ heavy-duty zipper

2 yards of ribbon

4 buttons 1″ in diameter (optional)

 TIP

Before you get started, preshrink the fabric. Make a small diagonal cut at the corners of each fabric near the selvages to prevent your fabric from fraying and tangling in the spin cycle. Then wash, dry, and press it.

june suggests

For my son's room I chose solid colors for the color blocking and then appliquéd his favorite T-shirts onto the center of each block. I used fusible web and a variety of cool stitches on the sewing machine.

cutting it out

Fabrics A–H

Fabric A: 1 rectangle 25″ × 37″

Fabric B: 1 square 34″ × 34″

Fabric C: 1 rectangle 10″ × 37″

Fabric D: 1 rectangle 16″ × 31″

Fabric E: 1 rectangle 16″ × 40″

Fabric F: 1 square 40″ × 40″

Fabric G: 1 rectangle 15″ × 31″

Fabric H: 1 rectangle 26″ × 31″

From the leftovers, cut 2 backing blocks 5″ × 18″ from any of Fabrics B, C, D, or G, and a total of 3 backing blocks 5″ × 18¾″ from Fabrics A and H.

Backing Fabrics

From your favorite of the 2 backing fabrics, cut 1 rectangle 40″ × 88″. From the other, cut 1 rectangle 27″ × 88″.

TIP

Keep in mind any directional prints as you sew the pieces together.

constructing it

All seam allowances are ½", fabrics are sewn right sides together, and all seams are pressed open unless otherwise noted.

Making the Duvet Top

1. Sew C to the long bottom edge of A. Press.

2. To make the top section, sew square B to the right-hand side of the A/C unit as shown. Press.

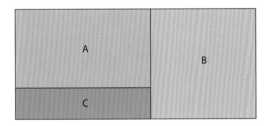

3. To make the middle section, sew E to D as shown. Press.

4. Sew G to the top of block H, press, and then sew the G/H unit to square F to complete the bottom section.

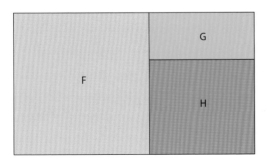

5. Sew the top, middle, and bottom sections together in order as shown, pressing after each addition.

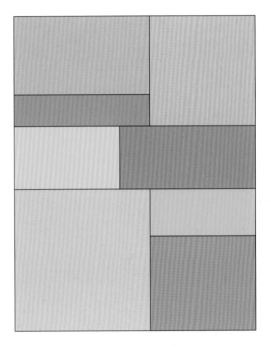

Making the Duvet Back

1. Sew the 5 backing pieces together along the short sides in any order. Press. Trim the backing strip to 5″ × 88″.

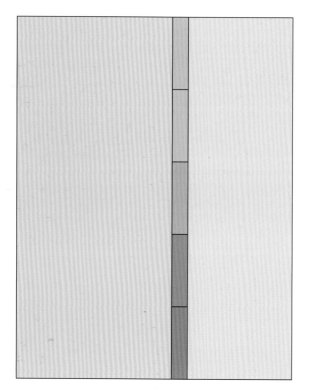

2. Sew the larger backing panel to the left side of the strip. Sew the smaller backing panel to the right side of the strip. Press.

3. On the wrong side of the duvet back, measure and mark with a pencil 17″ in from each bottom corner in the seam allowance.

putting it together

1. Pin the front and back of the duvet cover, right sides together, at the bottom. With the back panel right side up, sew from the right-hand corner to the 17″ mark, backstitching at the end of the seam. Clip the threads and sew the rest of the bottom of the duvet closed from the other 17″ mark to the corner, making sure to backstitch at the beginning of the seam.

2. Follow the manufacturer's instructions for installing a lapped zipper, with the overlap on the top side of the duvet cover. Make sure to open the zipper halfway so you can turn the duvet cover right side out later.

3. Pin the remaining 3 sides of the duvet front and back, right sides together, and stitch all around, pivoting at the 2 top corners. Make sure to overlap the bottom seam or backstitch at the beginning and end of this long seam.

4. From the ribbon, cut 4 lengths each 18″ long. Fold them in half and pin 1 ribbon, through the fold, at each corner of the duvet cover. Hand stitch in place at the fold, making sure your stitches won't show on the right side of the duvet cover.

5. Flip the duvet cover right side out and press the outside seams flat.

6. If the comforter doesn't have buttons or loops on each corner, hand stitch a button on each corner. Use the ribbons to tie the duvet cover to the comforter.

Cozy up with your little one and read a good book while wrapped up in the new linens.

Photos by Diane Pederson

shower curtain

Finished size: 36″ × 72″ per panel; makes 1 pair

A new shower curtain can make the entire bathroom feel new. With hundreds of pretty laminated cottons on the market you'll be able to find just the right fit for your decor. Match it up with a new set of towels and a rug, and you've made over the whole room.

Materials and Supplies

2 to 3 yards minimum of laminated cotton for main fabric, depending on orientation of pattern, plus more to match pattern repeat if desired

1½ yards laminated cotton for accent fabric, plus more to match pattern repeat if desired

1⅛ yards double-sided stiff fusible interfacing, 20″ wide, such as fast2fuse Light by C&T Publishing

12½ yards of ½″-wide double-fold bias tape

Extra-large eyelet kit

12 eyelets/grommets

ADDITIONAL TOOLS

Hole punch

june suggests

Home decor or lightweight canvas (instead of laminated cotton) would also make a great two-toned shower curtain.

cutting it out

Main Laminated Cotton

Trim off the selvages and be mindful of the print on the laminated cotton. Many laminated cottons have a distinct repeat, so lay out the fabric to determine the horizontal line that will be the top of both panels. You want the patterns to line up when the panels are hanging next to each other. Use a wide, clear ruler and a pencil to draw 2 panels that are 36″ × 53″ for the main sections of the 2 shower curtain panels. Cut using scissors or a rotary cutter and mat.

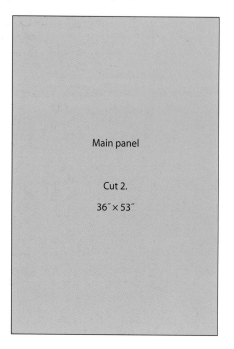

Main panel

Cut 2.

36″ × 53″

Accent Laminated Cotton

1. Again, being mindful of the fabric print, draw and cut out 4 rectangles 4½″ × 36″ for the headers.

2. Draw and cut out 2 rectangles 16½″ × 36″ for the bottoms of the panels, paying close attention to the fabric repeat. If you have a fabric with a strong vertical repeat, cut the panel bottoms to match the headers.

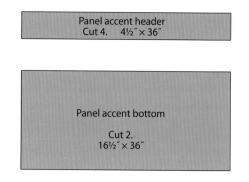

Panel accent header
Cut 4.   4½″ × 36″

Panel accent bottom

Cut 2.
16½″ × 36″

Interfacing

Cut out 4 headers 4″ × 36″.

sewing it up

Use a ½″ seam allowance unless otherwise stated.

1. Align the strips of interfacing with the tops of the headers. Following the manufacturer's instructions, fuse in place on the wrong side, leaving the bottom ½″ (seam allowance) void of interfacing. Be sure to protect your ironing board with parchment paper, an appliqué pressing sheet, or Silicone Release Paper (C&T Publishing).

2. Pin the bottom accent panel to the bottom of the main panel, right sides together, remembering to pin within the seam allowances. Sew together. Refer to *ironing laminated cotton* (page 15, in Tips and Tricks); using a pressing cloth and working with the wrong side up, press the seam allowances down toward the bottom accent panel.

3. With the wrong side up, edgestitch through the seam allowances, ⅛″ from the seam. Stitching from the wrong side of the laminated cotton will help avoid the pinching and pleating that can occur when topstitching on the laminated surface.

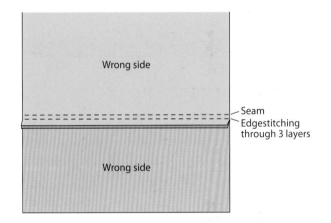

Wrong side

Wrong side

Seam
Edgestitching
through 3 layers

4. The headers are sewn to the main panels from the bottom edges. Layer the following 3 pieces and pin together within the bottom seam allowance:

- an interfaced header, right side up, with the seam allowance without interfacing at the top

- a main panel, right side up

- another header, wrong side up, with no interfacing at the top

Make sure that the seam allowance *minus interfacing* is at the top of the main panel. Interfacing would make this seam very bulky. Sew together.

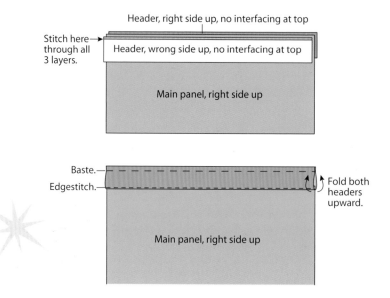

5. Fold the headers upward, encasing the raw edge at the top of the main panel, and press, making sure to use a pressing cloth because you will be ironing on the right side of the laminated cotton. Pin the headers together along the top edge.

6. Baste the top edge of the header closed; then edgestitch ⅛" away from the seam created in Step 4.

7. Refer to Bias Tape (page 17) to sandwich the double-fold bias tape around the shower curtain panel and stitch it in place, creating a mitered corner fold and finishing the overlap as you choose.

8. Create a template for the grommets/eyelets on paper by taping 4 pieces of paper together in a straight line; overlap them until they measure 36". Use your wide, clear ruler to draw a line 1" away from and parallel to the long edge. Mark a dot along the line 1" in from the corner.

9. Working from left to right, measure and mark a dot 6¾" from the previous dot on the 1" line. Repeat 4 times to mark 6 dots along the 1" line. Center a hole punch at each dot to create the finished template.

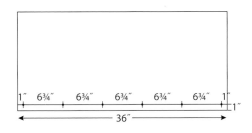

1" 6¾" 6¾" 6¾" 6¾" 6¾" 1" 1"

36"

10. Align the marked side of the paper template with the top of the header on the completed panel and mark the grommet placement with a pen. Follow the manufacturer's instructions to install the grommets.

11. Repeat Steps 2–10 to make the second curtain panel of the pair.

Taking a shower never looked so pretty!

candy knot guest towel

Finished size: 15" × 26" (may vary)

Don't you love getting out your best hand towels when company comes
a-callin'? Any basic hand towel from a bath department can be made pretty
with a whole lot of French knots. Don't be scared. French knots are like
meditation; just sit back and enjoy the quiet. Or better yet, turn on your
favorite TV drama. One band takes me about three hours to complete.

Materials and Supplies

Hand towel(s)*

Perle cotton embroidery thread #8 in 4–6 coordinating colors

ADDITIONAL TOOLS

Embroidery needles, size 9 or 10

Needle threader (*optional*)

Oval embroidery hoop, 5½" × 9"

Seam gauge

* Prewash the towel in case of shrinkage.

sewing it up

1. Slip an end of the towel right side up into the embroidery hoop. If the towel has a band, center it within the hoop.

2. Thread a needle with a strand of perle cotton. Prepping a few needles is helpful. For this project double the thread; slide the needle to the middle of the thread and knot the ends together.

3. Bring your needle up from the wrong side ¼" in from the right-hand edge of the towel. Refer to Hand Stitches (page 172) to make a French knot.

4. Angle the needle so it will come back up through the front of the towel ¼" to the left of the first French knot. Feel free to use a seam gauge to check your spacing. Make another French knot. If the knots are too close or too far apart, simply knot off and start over, removing any French knots that aren't to your liking.

5. Work from right to left until you have reached the end of the towel. Move the hoop when required.

6. When you get close to the end of the thread, knot off by bringing the thread to the back of the towel and putting the needle through a stitch. Wrap your needle twice around the thread and put the thread through to tighten it up. Clip off excess thread.

7. Choose a coordinating color for the next row to create a candy dot effect. Using the first row of knots as a guide, repeat the spacing.

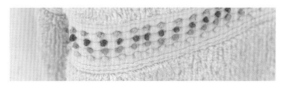

8. Repeat until the 2 bands are completed!

Now invite the girls over for cocktails so you can use your adorable new towel!

makeup tray

Finished size: 8″ long × 8″ wide × 2½″ high

Years ago, I received a fabric tray from my best neighbor friend as a gift. It was made of a pretty canvas fabric that always got dirty and dusty, but man, did it work well at holding my makeup. This pattern is inspired by that tray; my version is a different shape and made with oilcloth. Cleaning this one will be a breeze. Just wipe it clean, and let it air dry. Voilà—it's ready to use again.

measuring it

1. On a large sheet or roll of paper, draw a 13″ × 13″ square, using your wide, clear ruler (a roll of wrapping paper is a good size if you don't have pattern paper or craft paper); cut it out using paper-cutting scissors. Make sure that it's square; true up the pattern if need be. Fold the square into quarters.

2. Trace a curve on the outer, unfolded corner of the folded square with a circle stencil or a pot lid that is about 3″ in diameter. Cut on the curved line. Unfold your pattern and label it A.

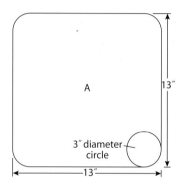

3. Repeat Step 1 to create a second square pattern. While it's still folded in quarters, measure and cut out a 2½″ square on the outer corner, through all 4 layers. When you open the pattern, you will have a fat plus-sign shape. Label this pattern B.

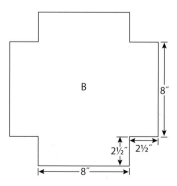

Materials and Supplies

2 fat quarters (18″ × 21″) oilcloth

½ yard nonfusible stiff interfacing, such as Timtex by C&T Publishing

1⅝ yards ½″-wide double-fold bias tape

4 buttons 1″ in diameter

cutting it out

1. From oilcloth fat quarters: Trace and cut out 1 Pattern A from each of the 2 fat quarters of oilcloth.

2. From interfacing: Trace and cut out 1 Pattern B.

sewing it up

1. Layer the A piece for the exterior of the tray right side down, then the B interfacing piece, centered, and then the A piece for the interior of the tray, right side up. Refer to *pinning oilcloth* (page 16, in Tips and Tricks) to pin the 3 pieces together along the outer ¼″ so you don't end up with puncture marks in the middle of the finished tray.

2. Machine-baste the layers together ⅛″ away from the edge, using a long basting stitch so that the oilcloth will move freely along the feed dogs.

3. Use your fingers to find the inner corners of the interfacing and mark them with pins. Don't pin through the interfacing—just catch the smallest amount of oilcloth that you can, so the pinholes will be incorporated into the stitches.

4. Place a strip of painter's tape on the sewing machine 2½″ away from the needle as a seam guide. Sew from pin to pin to create an 8″ × 8″ square in the center of each tray, pivoting with the needle down at each pin.

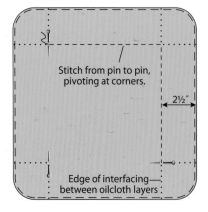

Stitch from pin to pin, pivoting at corners.

2½″

Edge of interfacing—between oilcloth layers

5. Refer to Bias Tape (page 17) to trim the outer edge of the tray with the ½″-wide cotton bias tape, finishing the ends as desired.

6. Place a pin where the interfacing stops on either side of a curved corner. Pinch the 2 adjacent sides of the tray together so the pins meet, pushing the uninterfaced corner inside the tray; this will create a pleat. Pin the corner together from the inside. Repeat until all 4 corners are pinned together.

7. Flip the tray inside out. Sew the top ½″ edge of each corner together at the pins, backstitching to secure.

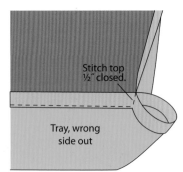

Stitch top ½″ closed.

Tray, wrong side out

8. Turn the tray right side out and slide your forefinger into the corner to round it out. Spread the bottom of each corner out slightly.

9. Hand stitch a button to each pleated corner so that it is centered on the bias trim. Hide the knot on the inside of the pleat by pushing the needle between the oilcloth and the button after your last stitch. Cut the thread leaving a 4″ tail; use this tail to create a knot, and snip it close.

Photo by Nissa Brehmer

Gather up your
makeup and
put it all in one
pretty place.

trimmed bed skirt

Finished size: customizable

Whether you're punching up an existing bed skirt or a brand new one, using a purchased one is a smart way to go. They come in so many styles and colors that it's easy to tie them in to your bedroom decor. So strip off that plain old bed skirt and make it nice and pretty! Instead of cutting individual bias strips and sewing them together, I'll walk you through how to make continuous bias binding.

Materials and Supplies

Purchased bed skirt

1 to 1¼ yards of quilting cotton for 2½"-wide single-fold bias trim

⅔ to ¾ yard of quilting cotton for ½"-wide double-fold bias trim

Bias tape maker (*optional*)

june suggests

Feel free to skip making your own bias binding and buy it premade. For the wider trim just look for wide single-fold bias online or at your local quilt shop. The smaller trim is ½"-wide double-fold bias that can be found nationwide at fabric shops and online.

calculating bias

The following chart tells you the length of continuous bias strips needed to cover the 3 sides of the skirt, how much yardage to buy, and what size square to cut from the fabric. I believe in having more than I need, so the length has about 30" added.

Bed Size	2"-wide bias strips for double-fold bias trim			5"-wide bias strips for single-fold bias trim		
	Length	Yardage	Cut Square	Length	Yardage	Cut Square
Twin	220"	2/3 yard	24" × 24"	220"	1 yard	34" × 34"
Full	235"	2/3 yard	24" × 24"	235"	1 yard	35" × 35"
Queen	250"	3/4 yard	26" × 26"	250"	1⅛ yards	36" × 36"
King	270"	7/8 yard	28" × 28"	270"	1⅛ yards	37" × 37"

making continuous bias strips

1. Trim the selvage edges from the fabric and cut a square according to the chart on page 104. A large clear ruler will help you make the corners neat and perfectly square.

2. Lay the square flat on the cutting mat, wrong side up, and mark the sides of the fabric with the number 1 near the middle. Then mark the top and bottom with the number 2 near the middle.

3. Fold the fabric in half diagonally, from point to point, and press a crease in the fabric. Unfold the fabric and cut along the 45° crease line. You now have 2 large triangles.

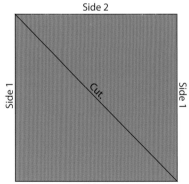

4. Lay the triangles on the table right side up and match up the sides labeled 1. Pin the triangles right sides together. Try to keep the little dog ears at either end even. Sew the seam together with a ¼" seam allowance and press it open.

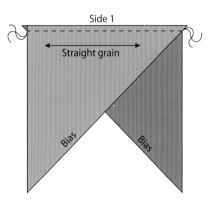

5. On the wrong side of the fabric, use a pencil or a fine-tip marker and a clear ruler to draw lines across the length of the fabric to make strips that are 2" or 5" wide. The longer the ruler, the quicker the work. Cut a few inches along the first line as shown at point A.

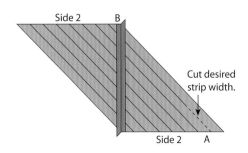

6. Bring the 2 short diagonal sides labeled 2 together, right sides facing. Offset the lines by 1 strip, matching points A and B as shown, and pin them together carefully to match up your drawn lines throughout.

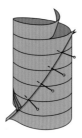

7. Sew another seam as shown, with a ¼" seam allowance, and press the seam open.

8. Continue cutting along the line as started in Step 5 to make a continuous bias strip.

9. Use a bias tape maker to fold the 2" bias strip into shape; follow the manufacturer's instructions and make sure not to stretch the bias when putting it through. If you don't have a bias tape maker, fold the bias strip in half lengthwise, wrong sides together, and press; fold the edges in to the center and press again.

10. Fold the 5"-wide bias strip in half lengthwise, wrong sides together, and finger-press a crisp crease in it. A little spray starch can help if you have it handy, and it gives the fabric a bit of added body.

sewing it up

1. Before you begin, make sure the bed skirt is clean and pressed per the manufacturer's recommendations. My bed skirt was new, and I chose not to prewash it, but I did give it a good ironing with steam and spray starch.

2. Pin the 5″-wide single-fold bias along the bottom edge of a long side of the bed skirt, leaving a 3″ tail at either end and aligning the raw edges of the bias tape with the bottom of the bed skirt. *Edgestitch* (page 14, in Tips and Tricks) the top of the bias tape to the bed skirt. Baste the lower edge in place.

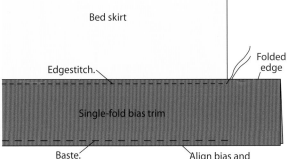

Bed skirt

Edgestitch.

Folded edge

Single-fold bias trim

Baste.

Align bias and bottom of bed skirt.

3. Repeat Step 2 on the other side and at the foot of the bed. If your bed skirt doesn't have split corners, you can trim the skirt with a single long seam. Fold over each 3″ tail back to the edge of the bed skirt and then behind the bed skirt, pressing and pinning in place. Refer to Hand Stitches (page 172) to slipstitch the tails down.

4. For the ½″-wide double-fold bias, sandwich the bias trim around the trimmed bottom of the bed skirt, leaving a 1″ tail at each end. Wrap the extra 1″ toward the back and tuck it neatly inside the fold of the bias trim. Pin and edgestitch in place, working your way around all sides as in Step 3. Trim the end of the bias to a 1″ tail and finish it off the same way you did at the beginning.

Now it's time to make your bed, grab a book, and enjoy the rest of your day in lovely style.

grr's crazy quilt

Finished size: 72" × 90"

I proudly possess a quilt that was handed down to me by my grandma, my Grr! It's a beloved family heirloom. I don't know how many times I've wrapped a sick child in it or how many movies we watched while cuddling under it. It's not fancy. No, it's not even pretty; it's ripped, torn, and stained—and I love every bit of its 1960s crazy-quilt madness. This is my version of the quilt that my Grr shipped to me for Christmas when I was cold and living 2,000 miles away from home for the first time. This pattern is made with as much love as Grr put into that care package nearly 20 years ago.

Materials and Supplies

⅓ yard each of 22 different fabric prints for quilt top (some leftovers will be used for the back)

2⅞ yards each of 2 fabrics for backing

¾ yard fabric for binding

2¾ yard batting, 90" wide*

1 ball of perle cotton #8

18" quilting hoop (*optional*)

* Choose a batting with a scrim when hand-tying a quilt like this; it will give the stitches more to bite into, and the quilt will hold up much better.

june suggests

For the most part my sample quilt is made with scraps and leftover fabric from all the Modern June aprons and the miscellaneous products that my Junies and I have made in the last seven years. Of course, you can use new fabric or use precut charm packs, perhaps filling in from your fabric stash and scraps.

cutting it out

WOF = width of fabric

1. From the quilt top fabrics: Cut 2 strips 5″ × WOF from each fabric. Subcut each strip into 8 squares 5″ × 5″ to yield a total of 352 squares. (You will use 320 for the top and 22 for the back, and have 10 extra.)

2. From the backing fabrics: Trim the selvages from both fabrics. Cut 1 rectangle 40″ × 99½″ from the first fabric. Cut 1 rectangle 34″ × 99½″ from the other fabric.

3. From the binding fabric: Cut 9 strips 2½″ × WOF.

june suggests

It's a quilter's choice to prewash the fabric or not; for this casual everyday quilt I opted not to.

sewing it up

Sewing Guidelines

All seam allowances are ¼″, and all seams are pressed to one side. Alternate the direction that you press the seams in each row to nest the seams and avoid bulky intersections.

Making the Quilt Top

1. Take some time to arrange your blocks into 20 stacks of 16 squares. Make sure that you don't have the same print in each pile twice. Try not to get too fussy about the order in which these are stacked; that helps make the quilt so charming. Remember, it's called a crazy quilt for a reason.

2. Refer to *chain stitching* (page 14, in Tips and Tricks) to chain piece 2 squares from a stack, right sides together, and then another 2 squares, without clipping the threads between. Repeat to sew all the squares in a stack into pairs.

3. Clip the threads between the pairs and continue to sew the pairs together until you have a row of 16 squares.

4. Repeat Steps 2 and 3 to make a total of 20 rows.

5. Lay the rows in front of you and spend a bit of time arranging them in order from top to bottom. Try to avoid having any of the same prints on top of each other.

6. When you have them in an order that you like, press the seam allowances in each row to alternating sides. Start with the bottom row, press to the right, and set the row aside. Working your way from the bottom to the top, alternate the direction of the seams. Stack one on top of the other. When you are finished, the top row will be on the top of the stack.

7. Pin the top 2 rows, right sides together, matching the seams. Sew. Press the seam allowances to the bottom.

8. Continue sewing rows in the same manner until all 20 rows are sewn together.

Photo by Diane Pederson

Making the Quilt Back

1. Arrange 22 of the remaining 5″ × 5″ squares in the order that you like best and sew them into a long strip.

2. Sew the 2 backing panels along the long sides of your block strip and press the seams to the side.

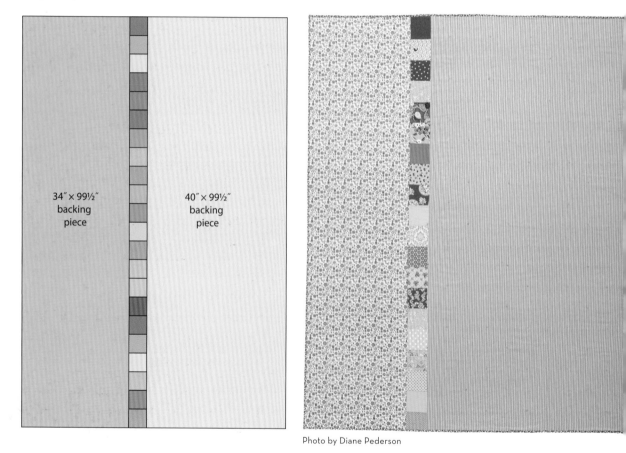

34″ × 99½″
backing
piece

40″ × 99½″
backing
piece

Photo by Diane Pederson

tying it up

1. On a clean, smooth floor, spread out the batting and place the quilt top on it, faceup. Smooth out any lumps and bumps. Cut your batting down so it's about 2" larger than the quilt top on each side.

2. Starting at the top of the quilt, carefully roll up the quilt top and batting as if it were a single piece and set it aside.

3. Spread the quilt backing onto the floor, wrong side up, smooth it out, and secure it to the floor with painter's tape. Tape it on all sides; use plenty of tape.

4. Roll the batting–quilt top combo onto the quilt backing, doing your best to center it. Insert a safety pin through all 3 layers every 2 blocks as shown by the red X's; baste the entire quilt this way.

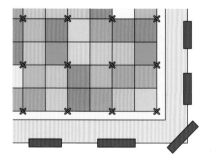

5. Remove and discard the tape. Turn the quilt over and make sure it is free of wrinkles. Carefully slide the quilt into a quilting hoop if you have one. You can also use a large embroidery hoop, or just stretch the quilt out over your lap.

6. Thread an embroidery needle with a single strand of perle cotton. You might want to use a needle threader. Pull your needle to the center of the thread, as if you were doubling it, but don't knot the ends. Prep several needles at once to save time and frustration later.

7. Leaving a 3" thread tail on the top of the quilt, take the needle down through a pinned corner, and with the opposite hand on the back of the quilt, feel for the needle and pull it through to the back. *Be careful not to pull the thread all the way out the back!* Guide the needle back up to the quilt top about ¼" away from its entry spot. Pull the thread taut, so that all 3 layers are securely bound.

8. Repeat the stitch for reinforcement. Stay close to the first stitch but avoid the same holes. Trim off all but 3" of the thread that is still attached to the needle.

9. Tie the 3" tails with a square knot twice. Trim the tails down to 1".

10. Repeat Steps 7–9 until you've replaced all the safety pins with knots, moving the hoop as needed. This will take some time, so gather up you girlfriends and put them to work.

11. Trim the backing and batting even with the edges of the quilt top.

binding it up

Sew the 2½"-wide binding strips, right sides together, with diagonal seams to make a continuous binding strip. Trim the seam allowance to ¼". Press the seams open.

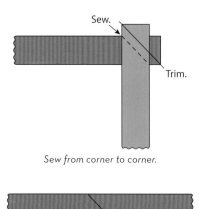

Sew from corner to corner.

Completed diagonal seam

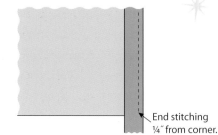

Figure 1. Stitch to ¼" from corner.

Press the entire strip in half lengthwise, wrong sides together. With raw edges even, pin the binding to the front edge of the quilt a few inches away from a corner, leaving the first few inches of the binding unattached. Start sewing, using a ¼" seam allowance.

Stop ¼" away from the first corner (see Figure 1), and backstitch a single stitch. Lift the presser foot and needle. Rotate the quilt a quarter turn. Fold the binding at a right angle so it extends straight above the quilt and the fold forms a 45° angle in the corner (see Figure 2). Then bring the binding strip down even with the edge of the quilt (see Figure 3). Begin sewing at the folded edge. Repeat in the same manner at all corners.

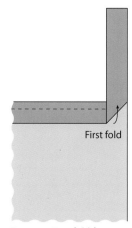

Figure 2. First fold for miter

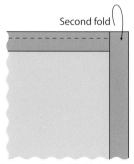

Figure 3. Second fold alignment

Continue stitching until you are back near the beginning of the binding strip. See Finishing the Binding Ends (page 115) for tips on finishing and hiding the raw edges of the ends of the binding.

Finishing the Binding Ends

Fold the ending tail of the binding back on itself where it meets the beginning binding tail. From the fold, measure and mark the cut width of your binding strip. Cut the ending binding tail to this measurement. For example, if your binding is cut 2½" wide, measure from the fold on the ending tail of the binding 2½" and cut the binding tail to this length.

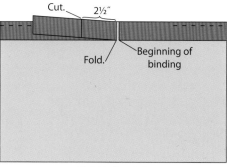

Cut binding tail.

Open both tails. Place a tail on top of the other tail at right angles, right sides together. Mark a diagonal line from corner to corner and stitch on the line. Check that you've done it correctly and that the binding fits the quilt; then trim the seam allowance to ¼". Press open.

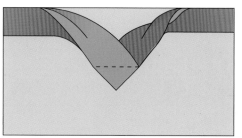

Stitch ends of binding diagonally.

Refold the binding and stitch this binding section in place on the quilt. Fold the binding over the raw edges to the quilt back and hand stitch. Have the girls back over, pop in a movie, and get everyone to help.

I hope that your crazy quilt will be part of family memories for generations to come!

casual roman shade

Finished size: customizable

When it comes to windows, I'm opinionated. I don't want fussy cornices or valances, and nothing is allowed to *swag*! It's just not my thing. I prefer white linen for shades and sheers. The quality of light that comes through white linen is bright and sunny. This is a casual, unlined Roman shade that is inset into the window trim. I've added some lovely ribbon to tie it in with my decor.

Materials and Supplies

Linen or linen/cotton blend fabric, 55" wide

1"-wide solid-colored ribbon

¾"-wide patterned ribbon or jumbo rickrack

Ring tape

Roman shade cording

½ yard of a thicker cord for pull

Cord condenser

Cord finial

2 cord cleats

1" × 2" wooden mounting board, cut to width of window

3 eye screws

1 wooden dowel rod, ¼" diameter

2 L-brackets, 1½" × 1½" × ½" (also called *corner braces* at some local hardware stores)

ADDITIONAL TOOLS

Electric drill or screwdriver

measuring it

A Roman shade requires only enough fabric to cover the window. There is no need for extra fullness, but we will add a small amount to the window's size for hems.

1. At the top of the window, measure the depth of the window. It must be at least ¾" to place the mounting board.

2. Measure the width and length of the inside of your window's frame. Insetting the Roman shade within the window creates a picture frame effect.

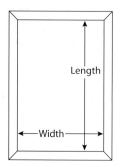

3. To determine the finished width of your shade, subtract ¼" from the width of your window. Doing so will keep the shade from rubbing when it is raised and lowered. If you have an old house like mine, you might want to check your window's width at multiple places. If it is not a uniform width, make the shade to fit the narrowest measurement.

4. Do the same to determine the shade's finished length, subtracting ¼" from the smallest measurement for the length.

5. Add 4" to the finished width of your window to determine the cut width for the shade.

6. Add 5" to the finished length to determine the cut length.

Use the measurements from Steps 5 and 6 to shop for the needed amounts of ribbons, ring tape, and fabric. You will need a little more than double the cut length of ribbons and ring tape per shade.

Example:
Measured window width:
$23˝ - ¼˝ = 22¾˝ + 4˝ = 26¾˝$ *cut width*

Measured window length:
$29˝ - ¼˝ = 28¾˝ + 5˝ = 33¾˝$ *cut length*

I would need 1 yard of fabric and 2 yards each of ribbons and ring tape per shade.

cutting it out

Linen

1. Prepare your fabric by cutting off the selvage edges.

2. On your prepared fabric, measure the cut width and length as determined in Measuring It, Steps 5 and 6. Pay close attention to the grain, making sure that your shade is on the straight-of-grain, and cut it out.

Ring Tape, Ribbons, and Cording

1. Cut 2 lengths of ring tape measuring 4" more than the finished length of the shade.

2. Cut 2 lengths of each ribbon or rickrack equal to the cut length of the shade.

3. Cut 1 length of the Roman shade cord the finished length of the shade plus 3". Cut a second length the finished length plus the finished width plus 3".

Mounting Board and Dowel

1. Cut down the 1" × 2" wooden mounting board to the finished width of your shade. Even though I have a shed full of tools, I prefer to have the kind folks at the local lumber yard or big-box hardware store do this job for me. No muss, no fuss—just a small cutting fee required.

2. Cut the dowel to the finished width minus ½".

constructing it

1. Pin a length of ¾"-wide ribbon or jumbo rickrack down the center of each length of 1"-wide ribbon. A clear ruler is very helpful for this step. Sew the pinned lengths together into a single unit. If you are using a ¾"-wide ribbon, sew down both sides of the smaller ribbon, near the edges. Rickrack can be sewn right down the center. Refer to Super H presser foot under *presser feet* (page 12, in Tools) for all you need to know about the Super H foot. It is ideal for both applications in this step.

2. Fold both long edges of the shade 1" toward the wrong side, press, and repeat to encase the raw edges. Do not pin or sew into place; you just want the crease lines for a guide at this time.

3. Repeat Step 2 on the bottom edge of the shade.

4. Open the side folds; pin both embellished ribbons in place on the right side of your fabric and *to the inside of each inner fold line* (this will be the outer edge of the shade). Edgestitch in place along both sides of the ribbon using a zipper foot. A little extra pinning is helpful and ensures that your ribbon goes on without wrinkles or tucks.

5. Pin the ring tape between the 2 fold lines on the right side of your fabric, making sure that the plastic rings are 1½" from the bottom of the shade. It's very important that both sides be even.

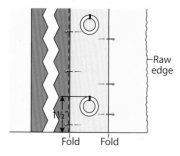

Raw edge

Fold   Fold

6. With the Super H foot, sew along both edges of the ring tape right along the creased fold lines. The foot should gently move the rings out of harm's way.

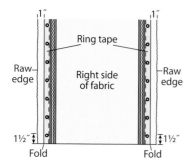

1"   1"
Ring tape
Raw edge   Right side of fabric   Raw edge
1½"   1½"
Fold   Fold

7. Fold along the crease lines again to fold both of the side hems to the wrong side of the shade, encasing the raw edges within the folds. *Slipstitch* (page 172, in Hand Stitches) the folds closed, making sure your stitches don't show on the front of the shade.

8. Lay the shade wrong side up and fold the bottom hem up, enclosing the raw edges of the ribbon and ring tape. Unstitch any rings that might end up in the hem. At the corners, cheat the hem in at a slight angle. Pin the hem from side to side and edgestitch it closed using the Super H foot, or slipstitch it by hand. Leave the sides of the hem open to create a pocket for the dowel.

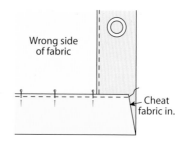

Wrong side of fabric

Cheat fabric in.

9. Handstitch the bottommost rings back onto the corners at the top of the hem, if needed. Do not sew through all the layers. Slide the dowel through the hem pocket created in the previous step.

installing it

1. With a disappearing-ink pen draw a line that is 3″ from the top raw edge of the shade. Align the line with the top edge of the mounting board, with the wrong side of the fabric toward the board, as shown below. Staple the fabric across the narrow top edge of the board. Next, wrap the fabric around to the bottom of the board and secure with more staples.

2. Attach the 3 eye screws into the back of the board, through the fabric—the first in the center, the other 2 about 1″ in from the ends of the board. Then screw the L-brackets to the edge of the board as shown, just inside the screw eyes.

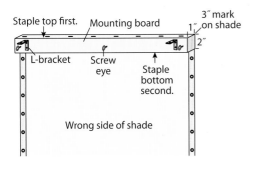

3. Lay the Roman shade facedown on a table, so it is smooth and wrinkle free. Tie the cut Roman shade cords to the bottom rings with a double knot, and then thread the cords up through the rings and the closest screw eye. Decide which side of the shade will have the shade pull (*remember, you are working backward*) and run the cord from the side opposite the shade pull through the center screw eye and the screw eye nearest the shade pull.

4. After the cords are even and have no slack, place a cord condenser 3″ from the edge of the mounting board as shown at right. Follow the

manufacturer's instructions to attach the cord condenser and finial, using the thicker cord for the bottom pull.

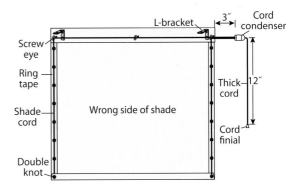

5. Screw the mounting board up through the L-brackets into the bottom of the upper portion of the window casing. Then, attach 2 cord cleats to the outside of the window trim—the first up high so you can keep the cords up and out of the way, and the second down low so you can wind up the pull cord when the shade is up.

Important Note on Safety

Please research the latest safety requirements for more information on cording if you have or care for small children. As of the publication of this book this pattern is up to standard. Rings must be no more than 8″ apart, and all cords must be condensed into one short cord or left loose so that they can't harm a child at play.

lined baskets

Finished size: customizable

Who doesn't love a good basket? Wire, wicker, or wooden; vintage or brand new—they keep life neat and tidy. So why not spruce them up! Make them pretty—and practical!

Materials and Supplies

Basket(s)

Laminated cotton for exterior and interior

Interfacing

Double-fold bias tape

june suggests

This is another project that you could use almost any type of fabrics for, from quilting cotton to oilcloth. I've chosen to use laminated cotton because it's easy to clean; closets and pantries can get dusty over time. Every once in a while I wipe down the laminated liners with a damp cloth, and I'm done.

cutting it out

1. This pattern will lead you through how to make a lining for a basket that is wider at the top than at the bottom. When sizing the basket for the lining, measure the inside of the basket to get the right fit. Using a flexible measuring tape, find the length (A) and width (B) along the top and then along the bottom (D and E) of the basket. Then measure the depth (C) of the basket.

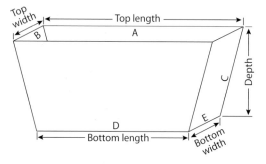

2. Use the measurements taken in Step 1 to create your own pattern. Refer to *pattern paper* (page 12, in Tips and Tricks) for suitable pattern paper. On a large piece of paper, using a wide, clear ruler and a pencil, draw a rectangle (or square) according to the bottom length (D) and width (E) measure-ments. Mark the center of all 4 sides. Cut out the rectangle on the drawn lines.

The bottom of my smallest basket is 6˝ × 8˝; I drew a rectangle the same size.

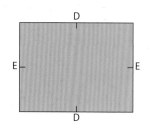

3. Along the bottom of another piece of paper, draw a line the length of the basket bottom (D) and mark the center. From the center point of D, draw a perpendicular line straight up that is the same length as the basket's depth (C).

My basket is 8˝ in length and 7˝ tall, so I drew a line 7˝ high, centered on the D line.

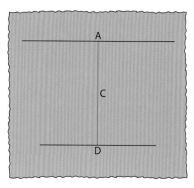

4. At the top of C, and centered on it, draw a perpendicular line the length of the top of the basket (A).

My basket is 10½˝ along the top, so I drew a 10½˝ line (5¼˝ to either side of C) that was parallel to the bottom length.

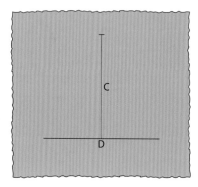

5. Now connect the ends of the 2 parallel lines to create 2 diagonal lines that will be the side seams for the basket liner pattern.

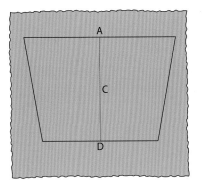

6. To create the fold-over for the basket liner, draw a third parallel line, 2½″ to 4½″ above the A line, and as long as A. The bigger the basket, the deeper the fold-over should be.

For my small basket I chose to go with a 2½″ fold-over, and for the larger basket shown I went with a 4½″ fold-over.

7. If you're working off a paper roll, cut your drawing paper away from the roll. Leave a good 2″ on either side of your drawing for future steps. Cut the excess paper away above the fold-over line drawn in Step 6.

8. Fold the paper, blank sides together, along line A. With the drawn side of the pattern up, use a *tracing wheel* (page 13, in Tools) to transfer the angle of the side seams onto the fold-over. Unfold the pattern and trace the perforated line with a pencil on the right side. These 2 lines are the fold-over side seams.

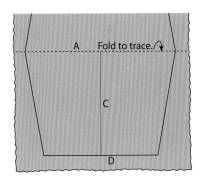

☞ TIP

If you don't have a tracing wheel, simply fold the portion of the fold-over pattern that shows back over the angled side seams to mark their placement.

9. Using the clear ruler, add ¾″ to each diagonal line as shown (¼″ for seam allowance and ½″ to add some ease to the pattern).

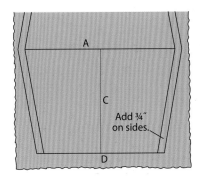

10. Fold the pattern in half along the C line to check that it is symmetrical. If it's off in any way, remeasure and make any adjustments. When the pattern is trued up, cut it out, trace it, and cut out a second copy.

11. Repeat Steps 3–10 for the basket's smaller side, using the widths (B and E) and the depth (C).

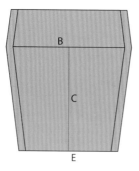

12. Tape the base and the 4 side pieces together as shown to create the finished basket liner pattern, matching the bottom lengths (D) and widths (E) and the center marks. The seam allowances will overlap at the D/E intersections, but that's okay.

13. To determine the amount of fabric needed, measure the pattern from top to bottom and side to side. Rotate the pattern to find the most efficient way to cut it out. Buy the same amount of 2 coordinating laminated cotton prints for a two-toned effect, or double the amount if you want to use the same print for the interior and exterior of the liner.

14. Cut out 2 basket liners using your pattern, 1 for the interior and 1 for the exterior.

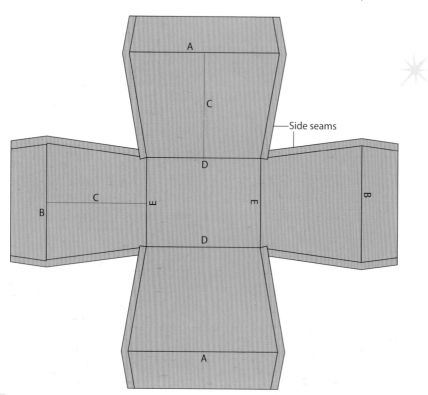

sewing it up

1. On the interior basket liner piece, pin 2 adjacent angled sides, right sides together, at the top corners. It's normal if the angles from the small and the large sidewalls vary slightly; just bring the corners together at the top and align the sides to create the right shape for your basket. Sew them together using a ¼" seam allowance, pivoting at the fold-over point and backstitching at the top. Repeat to sew all 4 side seams to create a boxlike shape.

2. Refer to *ironing laminated cotton* (page 15, in Tips and Tricks) to press the seams to the side, using a pressing cloth to protect your material from the heat of the iron.

3. Repeat Steps 1 and 2 to make the exterior of the basket liner.

4. Slide the interior of the liner inside the exterior, wrong sides together. Match up the side seams and pin the 2 pieces together along the top raw edge. Baste around the raw edge if desired.

5. Refer to Bias Tape (page 17) to sandwich the double-fold bias tape around the raw edge of the basket liner, edgestitching it in place and finishing the ends as desired.

6. Slide the finished basket liner into the basket. Slowly and carefully turn the fold-over down over the top of the basket. This will be a snug fit; to avoid ripping the stitches, pull about ½" of the liner over each corner to start with and then slowly pull the rest down.

For my small basket I made sure that I had an even 2″ folded over.

Your amazing baskets are now ready to be filled. You'll be making these for every room of the house—I just know it.

clothespin bag

Finished size: 12″ × 13″

Don't you love to hang the sheets outside on a gorgeous summer day? This fun pattern will help corral the pins—or pegs—in a pretty and practical place.

Materials and Supplies

4 coordinating fat quarters (18″ × 21″)

1¼ yards ½″-wide double-fold bias tape

Small scrap of double-sided fusible web

Child-size clothes hanger

june suggests

If you like the idea of leaving your clothespin bag outside all summer long, then switch to an outdoor fabric. These fabrics are mold- and fade-resistant, so they can weather the elements.

preparing it

Enlarge the clothespin bag pattern (page 130) by 200%, copy or trace onto card stock, and cut it out. If you're tracing, make sure to copy *all* the lines and markings onto the pattern.

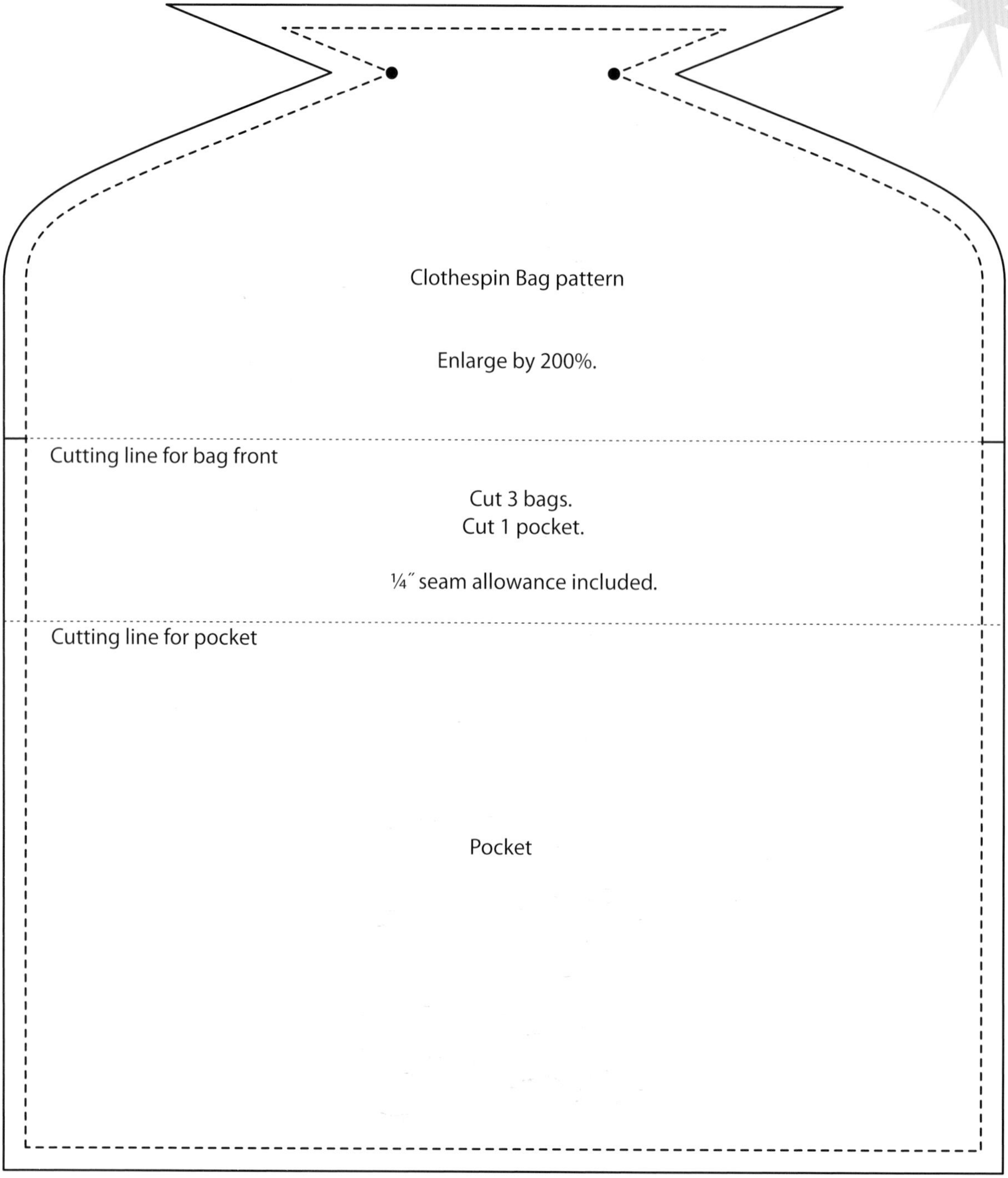

Clothespin Bag pattern

Enlarge by 200%.

Cutting line for bag front

Cut 3 bags.
Cut 1 pocket.

¼″ seam allowance included.

Cutting line for pocket

Pocket

☞ **TIP**

Use a pair of pinking shears to cut out all the pieces
to quickly finish off your seams.

Fat Quarters A and B

Choose 2 fat quarters—a fabric for the back of the bag and a fabric for the
back lining (you won't see very much of this fabric in the finished bag). Layer
the 2 fat quarters, right sides together, with the lining piece on top. Trace the
outside of the full pattern and the dots at the top onto the wrong side of the
lining. Make sure to orient any directional prints correctly. Cut out both pieces.

Fat Quarter C

1. Trace the full pattern on the wrong side of the fat quarter you want for the
front of the bag. Mark the dots as in the previous step and the horizontal bag
front cutting line across the bag. Cut out the bag front.

2. Cut the bag front along the horizontal line into 2 pieces—a top and bottom
bag front.

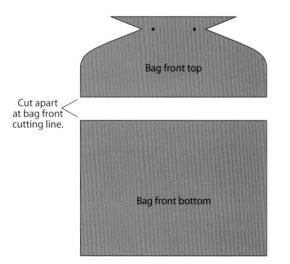

Cut apart
at bag front
cutting line.

Bag front top

Bag front bottom

Fat Quarter D

Fold the pattern on the pocket line, trace only the lower half onto the wrong
side of the remaining fat quarter, and cut it out.

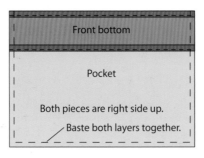

sewing it up

1. Refer to Bias Tape (page 17) to sandwich and edgestitch the ½″-wide double-fold bias tape on the upper edges of the pocket and the bottom bag front, and the lower edge of the top bag front. You can use purchased bias tape or make your own. Trim the ends of the bias tape even with the sides of the pieces.

2. Layer the pocket onto the bottom bag front, both right sides up. Pin and baste the 2 pieces together along the sides.

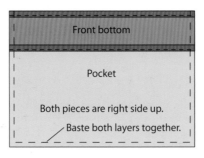

Front bottom

Pocket

Both pieces are right side up.

Baste both layers together.

3. Layer the bag back lining, wrong side up; the bag back, right side up; and the basted bag bottom front / pocket unit, wrong side up. Align these 3 pieces at the bottom corners. Place the top bag front at the top of the layered pieces, also wrong side up. Align all the pieces at the top, and pin and baste all the layers together.

4. Using a ¼″ seam allowance, stitch the bag together from dot to dot all around the edges, leaving the top open and backstitching at the beginning and end, and along the sides of the bag front opening, over the bias tape.

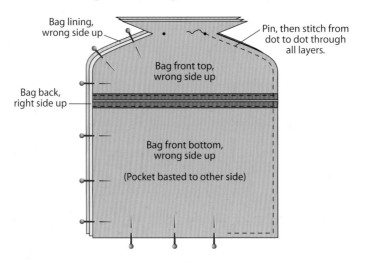

Bag lining, wrong side up

Pin, then stitch from dot to dot through all layers.

Bag front top, wrong side up

Bag back, right side up

Bag front bottom, wrong side up

(Pocket basted to other side)

5. Fold the loose end piece at the top of the bag front over to the wrong side and press flat. This creates a hem at the top opening for the clothes hanger. Cut a piece of fusible web 1″ × 8″, remove any paper backing, and slide it up into the fold. Cut off any excess tape. Iron the hem closed.

6. Repeat Step 5 on the other side of the bag, folding over both the back and back lining together as a single piece.

7. Trim and clip the seam allowances of the 2 bottom corners and along the curves. Serge or zigzag the seam allowances to finish them, if you want. Turn the bag right side out through the front opening and press; be sure that the seams are flat and the corners are sharp.

8. Sewing 1/2″ in from each side of the bag, stitch over the 2 rows of bias trim at the upper opening, backstitching at the beginning and end. This will hide the seam allowances on the inside of the bag and add strength to the opening.

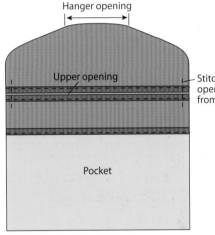

Hanger opening

Upper opening

Stitch over opening 1/2″ from each side.

Pocket

Your bag is ready to be filled with clothespins, and you are ready to hang the laundry in vintage style!

plastic bag holder

Finished size:

5″ diameter × 13″ long

Plastic bags! We love to hate them, don't we? Even though they are a nuisance, they can be handy to have around. This useful tube-shaped bag can help to keep them under control.

Materials and Supplies

½ yard laminated cotton main fabric for the exterior

⅝ yard laminated cotton accent fabric for the lining and bottom

¼ yard lightweight double-sided fusible stiff interfacing, 20″ wide, such as fast2fuse Light by C&T Publishing

1 yard ½″-wide grosgrain ribbon

june suggests

Make one without a hole at the bottom and you've got a cute trash can for your car!

preparing it

Trace the bag pattern on page 136 onto the interfacing with a pencil. (If you can't see the pattern lines through your interfacing, trace the pattern onto thin paper, cut that out, and trace around the inner and outer edges onto the interfacing.) Roughly cut out the interfacing around the outside circle.

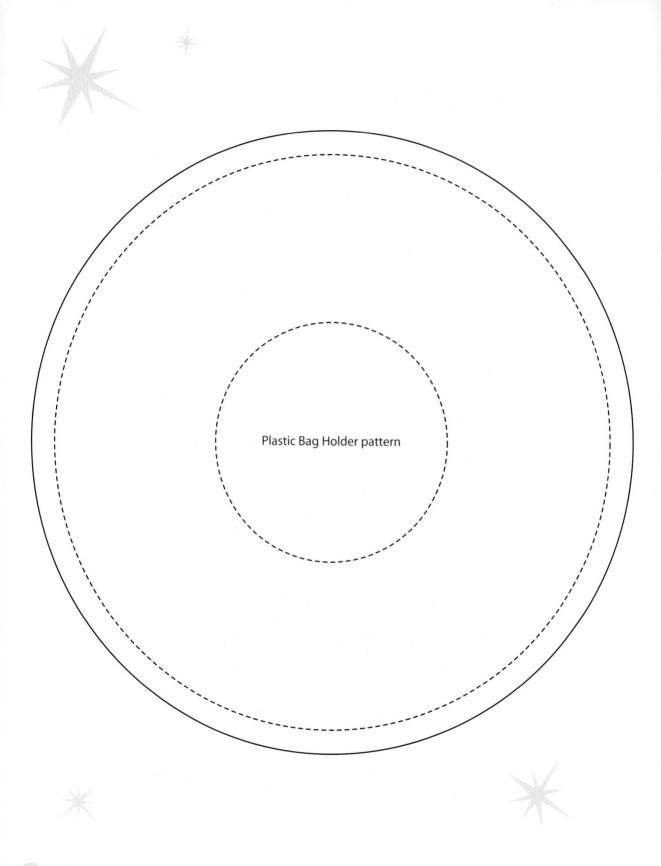

Plastic Bag Holder pattern

cutting it out

1. Cut 2 squares 9″ × 9″ from the accent fabric for the bag bottom and bag bottom lining. Refer to *ironing laminated cotton* (page 15, in Tips and Tricks) and follow the manufacturer's instructions to fuse the traced interfacing, centered, to the wrong side of a 9″ × 9″ square. Remember that this is double-sided fusible, so use parchment paper, an appliqué pressing sheet, or Silicone Release Paper (by C&T Publishing) to keep the side without the fabric from being fused at this point. Layer the 9″ × 9″ squares, right sides together, and pin them together inside the inner circle.

2. On the exterior fabric, use a wide, clear ruler to draw and cut out a 13″ × 18⅞″ rectangle for the bag body.

3. On the lining fabric, draw and cut out a rectangle 18⅞″ × 20″ for the bag body lining. Cut out the lining. On the wrong side of the lining, draw a pencil line 3½″ down from the top edge. Mark 5″ in from the edges on the line.

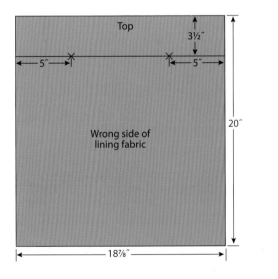

4. Cut 2 pieces of grosgrain ribbon, both 18″ long. Seal the edges with seam sealant such as Fray Check.

sewing it up

1. With the interfacing side up, stitch the inner circle of the bag base, right on the line.

2. Use a pair of snips to cut out the inside of the small inner circle, leaving a ¼" seam allowance. Clip the seam allowance all around. Use scissors to cut through all 3 layers on the outermost line.

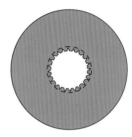

3. Turn the bag base right side out. Baste the outer edge of the circle closed, using a long stitch ⅛" from the edge. *Making sure to use a pressing cloth,* fuse the other side of the bag base.

4. Gently fold the bag base in quarters, place a pin at each fold to mark it, and set aside.

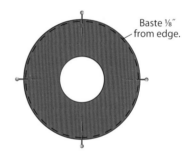

Baste ⅛"
from edge.

5. Push a pin through the 5" marks on the wrong side of the bag lining to the front. Pin an end of each trimmed ribbon ½" above the line at the pin on the right side.

6. Align the tops of both the lining and exterior rectangles, right sides together with the lining fabric on top, and pin on the stitching line 3½" down from the top. The lining fabric will be 7" longer at the bottom. With the lining side up, sew a seam along the pencil line, catching the bottom ends of the ribbon ties in the seam.

7. Refer to *ironing laminated cotton* (page 15, in Tips and Tricks) to press the wide seam allowance up toward the lining fabric, making sure to use a pressing cloth.

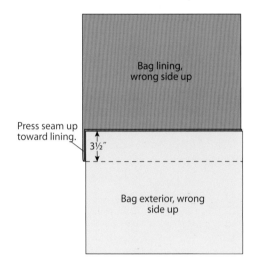

Bag lining, wrong side up

Press seam up toward lining.

3½″

Bag exterior, wrong side up

8. Bring the 2 long side seams together, pin, and sew using a ¼″ seam allowance to make a long tube.

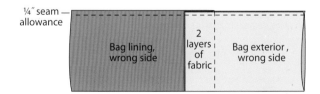

¼″ seam allowance

Bag lining, wrong side

2 layers of fabric

Bag exterior, wrong side

9. Carefully press the seam allowance to the side without creasing the fabric tube. A sleeve board or sleeve roll is handy for this step but not necessary. You can also roll up a towel and slip it inside the tube.

10. Fold the lining down outside the tube until the bottom edges of both fabrics match up (the layers should be wrong sides together now). Pin the 2 layers together around the bottom of the bag and baste ⅛″ from the raw edges. Starting at the tube seam, repeat Step 4 to mark the bottom of the bag tube in quarters.

11. With the tube lining side out, match and pin together the tube and the bag base, making sure that the spacing is even and smooth. Sew together with a ¼″ seam allowance. Use a stiletto or other narrow pointed object to flatten and smooth any pleats and tucks as you sew. This is a slow process; be patient and careful.

12. Press the top edge of the bag, using a pressing cloth, and then *bar tack* (page 14, in Tips and Tricks) the ribbons to the top edge.

13. Tie the ribbons into a bow.

Hang your pretty and practical bag on a hook or doorknob and start filling it up!

giant mood board

Finished size: 48″ × 84″
(customizable)

Read any design or decor blog and you'll know that mood boards are oft used and quite popular. And I say go big or go home! Take a trip to a lumber or hardware store for a piece of fiberboard sheathing and make a stop at a local home decor fabric shop, and you soon will have a great way to organize your next big design project.

Materials and Supplies

Quantity of materials required will vary based on desired size of mood board.

- -

4′ × 8′ sheet of ½″-thick fiberboard sheathing, cut to size(s) desired

- -

Canvas, linen, or ticking fabric (You may need wide fabric if you are planning on a large mood board.)

- -

⅜″-wide grosgrain ribbon, equal to the perimeter of your board plus 4 times its height

- -

1″-wide grosgrain ribbon, equal to the perimeter of your board

- -

ADDITIONAL TOOLS

- -

Staple gun and ¼″ staples

- -

Screwdriver and 4 drywall screws, 1″ long

cutting it out

Fiberboard Sheathing

1. After you have chosen a place for your mood board, decide its height and width based on your available wall space. The wall above my sewing machine measures 51″ × 91″, so I opted for a mood board that would be 48″ × 84″. The sheathing comes in 4′ × 8′ (48″ × 96″) panels, so consider that as well.

2. Take the measurements for your mood board(s) to a hardware store and have the sheathing cut to the size(s) that you need. You can get multiple smaller mood boards from a 4′ × 8′ panel. The store might charge you a small fee for cutting the board, but it's worth the cost.

Fabric

1. Add 6″ to the height and length of your mood board to determine your fabric cut size. Depending on the orientation of your board, the height of your board may be the width or the length of your fabric. Divide the larger number by 36 to determine the yardage you need to buy.

> *Example:*
> *48″ + 6″ = 54″ cut width;*
> *84″ + 6″ = 90″ cut length;*
> *90″ ÷ 36 = 2.5 yards, so I would buy 2½ yards, or 2¾ yards if I want a little extra.*

2. Cut your fabric to the size determined in the previous step.

stapling it

1. Prep the fabric by ironing out any creases; a hot steam iron and bit of spray starch might be helpful.

2. Lay the ironed fabric, right side down, onto a large, sturdy table; center the fiberboard on top. If using fabric with a loose weave, make sure the fiberboard is placed on grain to keep any fabric print running evenly on the board.

3. Starting at the top, staple the fabric to the board in the center of the side. Move to the bottom of the board, pulling the fabric taut, and staple the fabric in place several times in the center.

4. Flip the board to see that the fabric is smooth and straight. If you are using patterned fabric, check its positioning. If you are not happy with it, remove the staples, reposition the board, and repeat Steps 1–3 as needed.

5. Staple the fabric on an adjacent side at the center, and then staple at the center of the opposite side. Just as you did in the previous step, check the front to make sure that all is looking right on the front.

6. After the fabric is stapled along all 4 sides near the center, staple from the center outward along the long sides, placing the staples 2″–3″ apart, and then finish stapling the short sides.

7. At each corner, fold the fabric in to make a right angle; staple it in place twice.

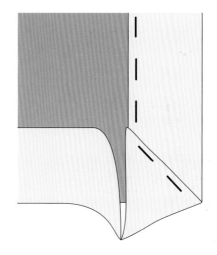

8. Fold the fabric at each corner in a second time, vertically, about 1″ from the edge, and staple in place.

june suggests

This stapling project is slightly different from the others in the book because of the material that we are using. The softer fabrics don't need to be cut down at the corners in the same way.

making the ribbon border

1. Using a disappearing-ink pen and a clear, gridded ruler, on the right side of the mood board draw a rectangle 2″ in from the outer edge. Draw a second rectangle 4″ in from the outer edge (or 2″ inside the rectangle you just drew).

2. Pin the ⅜″-wide ribbon on top of the outer drawn rectangle, using clear pushpins to secure it at the corners and as needed to keep it from sagging. Overlap the ribbon by 1″ where the ends meet, pin in place, and trim. Repeat on the inner drawn rectangle with the 1″-wide ribbon. Pushpins allow you to rearrange or change your ribbon borders when you change the mood board.

3. For this project I divided the main part of the board into 5 equal sections and cut 4 pieces of ⅜″-wide ribbon to this length. I pinned the ribbons in place under the top inner ribbon border and tucked them under the bottom inner border.

hanging it up

The fiberboard sheathing is lightweight and easy to screw into. Attach the board to a wall by driving 4 screws through the board and into a stud in the wall. You can cover up the hardware with the ribbon borders or with photos.

Get inspired! And be inspired. If you like it, put it on your board. This is the original Pinterest— and it's tangible!

june suggests

Don't forget all those extra fiberboard sheathing panels; they would be great for the kids' rooms and to help you keep organized in the kitchen.

ironing table

Finished size: customizable • **Pocket panel:** 4½" × 7¾"

Let's get creative with our ironing space. This project can turn any flat surface into an ironing station. So look around your craft/sewing room; maybe a bookshelf or dresser can be retrofitted into an ironing table. By doing so, you can eliminate your ironing board and make room for something new. Don't have a permanent craft room? You can still make this and stash it between uses.

Materials and Supplies

Quantity of materials required will vary based on size of table.

Table, dresser, or bookshelf that is counter height

¾"-thick plywood, cut to fit tabletop

Cotton canvas, twill, or heavyweight home decor fabric for ironing table cover

Metalized Mylar insulated interfacing, 45" wide, such as Insul-Fleece by C&T Publishing

⅜ yard ½"-wide double-fold bias tape

Hook-and-loop tape (*optional*)

ADDITIONAL TOOLS

Staple gun and ¼" staples

june suggests

Set up an L-shaped sewing station with your sewing machine on one side and the ironing table on the other. If they are all on the same level, you'll never have to jump up to iron again!

cutting it out

Plywood

1. Measure the width and length of your new ironing table.

2. If you don't have the time, ability, or resources to cut the wood yourself, go to a hardware store and have the staff cut a piece of ¾"-thick plywood to the measurements in Step 1. It's so quick and easy, you might consider this even if you have the resources.

Insulated Interfacing

1. Add 6" to both the width and the length of the tabletop measurements to determine the cut size of the insulated interfacing. Double that amount to determine the total amount you will need to buy.

My table measures 20˝ × 36˝, so I needed 2 pieces of interfacing, each 26˝ × 42˝. Since Insul-Fleece is sold in a Craft Pack of 1 piece 27˝ × 45˝, I needed 2 packages.

2. Cut 2 pieces of insulated interfacing to the size determined in the previous step.

Insul-Fleece

Canvas

1. Cut 1 piece of the ironing board cover fabric to the same cut size as the insulated interfacing. A sturdier fabric will hold up nicely under the heavy use of ironing.

2. You'll need an extra ¼ yard of fabric for the pocket unit, but this could be a different fabric. Use a clear, gridded ruler to mark and cut the following pieces:

> 1 rectangle 5″ × 4″ for the bottom pocket
>
> 1 rectangle 5″ × 6″ for the top pocket
>
> 2 rectangles 5″ × 10″ for the backing

stapling it

Insulated Interfacing

1. Refer to Bench Redo, Stapling It, Steps 1–4 (page 58), to staple both layers of insulated interfacing together as a single layer onto the cut plywood. You only need to staple twice on each side.

2. At a corner of the plywood, fold the corner of the interfacing inward and staple it in place across the corner, about 1″ away from the point. Cut the interfacing off diagonally.

3. Fold the loose interfacing in to the center from either side of the corner at a 45° angle. With a marker, draw a line along the 45° fold line. Unfold and cut the interfacing away from between the marker line and the corner of the board. Butt the cut edges up against each other and staple in place.

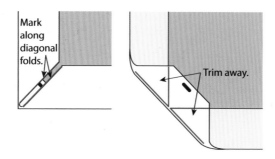

Mark along diagonal folds.

Trim away.

4. Repeat Steps 2 and 3 on the remaining corners.

Canvas

1. Repeat Steps 1 and 2 of the insulated interfacing process for the canvas.

2. Fold the extra fabric neatly at the corners (instead of trimming it) and staple the folds in place.

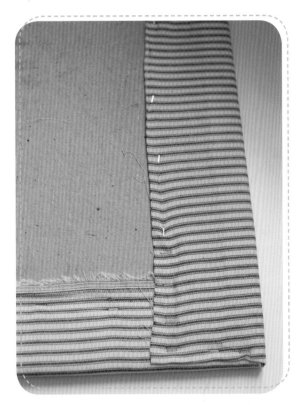

3. Continue stapling the canvas all the way around the plywood. Keep the staples closer together for the canvas, about 2″ apart.

sewing it up

1. Refer to Bias Tape (page 17) to trim the top 5″ edge of the 2 pockets with the double-fold bias tape. Trim the edges of the tape flush with the sides of the pockets.

2. Place a 5″ × 10″ pocket backing piece right side up. Pin the larger pocket, right side up, and then the smaller pocket, right side up, at the bottom of the backing, aligning the raw edges. Baste around the sides and bottom of the 2 pockets.

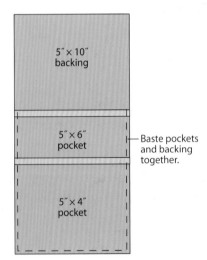

3. Pin the remaining backing piece to the pinned-together pocket unit, right sides together, along both sides and the bottom, making sure to leave the top free. Sew the 3 pinned sides together using a ¼″ seam allowance.

4. Clip the corners and turn the pocket right side out, as you would a pillowcase. Use a long point turner or chopstick to push the corners out.

5. Iron the pocket so that the seams are even and flat and the corners are sharp. Baste the top of the pocket closed.

6. With the ironing table upside down, place the pocket unit wrong side up so that it's hanging from the left corner as shown if you are right-handed. Put it on the opposite corner if you're a lefty. Position the pocket panel about 1″ from the side and 2″ in

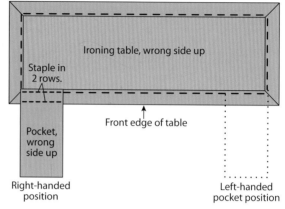

Ironing table, wrong side up

Staple in 2 rows.

Pocket, wrong side up

Front edge of table

Right-handed position

Left-handed pocket position

from the front edge. Attach the pocket to the table with 2 rows of staples— the first close to the edge of the wood and the second near the top edge of the pocket unit.

setting it up

Turn it over!

The weight of the thick plywood should keep the ironing table from sliding around. If you need a more permanent solution, you could attach adhesive hook-and-loop tape to the bottom of the plywood and to the top of your furniture, but it may affect the finish of the furniture.

You're ready to make more of my Modern June patterns on your new ironing table.

sewing machine cover

Finished panel: 24½" × 42" (customizable)

We don't always get to sew as much as we'd like. It's sad when dust spends more time on your sewing machine than you do. Not only does it prove how long it's been since you last sewed a stitch, but it's not good for your machine. This pretty little sewing machine cover is filled with helpful pockets. Keep the sewing machine manual in the large one and your tools in the small ones.

Materials and Supplies

Yardage will vary slightly depending on the size of your sewing machine.

Approximately ½ yard quilting fabric for exterior

Approximately ½ yard quilting fabric for lining

2 coordinating fat quarters for pockets

Approximately 1½ yards of lightweight woven fusible interfacing, such as Shape-Flex by C&T Publishing

1 or 2 packages ½"-wide double-fold bias tape

2 yards of grosgrain ribbon

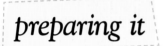

preparing it

1. Measure the widest part of your sewing machine from side to side and add 1".

My machine is 15" wide so my pattern measurement will be 16" across.

2. Now measure from front to back over the machine, including its deepest part, for the length of the cover.

My home sewing machine is 29".

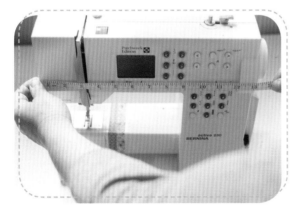

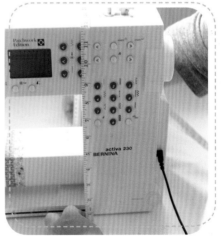

3. Draw a rectangle with these measurements onto the wrong side of the lining fabric using a wide, clear ruler. Place the longer measurement of your cover parallel with the selvage edge of the fabric so that the fabric is on grain, and make sure all 4 corners are square.

4. Use the width measurement from Step 1 to draft the large pocket. On the back of a fat quarter, draw a rectangle 9" × Step 1 width.

My large pocket pattern is 9˝ × 16˝.

5. For the small pocket, on the back of another fat quarter, draw a rectangle 2" shorter than the last, by the same width.

My small pocket is 7˝ × 16˝.

6. To determine how much double-fold bias tape you will need to buy or make, add the length and width of the cover rectangle and multiply by 2 to determine the perimeter of your cover. Add a few extra inches to join the ends, and divide by 36 to determine yardage.

Example:
16˝ + 29˝ = 45˝ × 2 = 90˝ + extra; so I need 2⅝ yards.

cutting it out

1. Layer the exterior fabric, 2 layers of interfacing, and the lining fabric, marked side up. Pin all 4 layers together and cut out the cover rectangle from all 4 layers.

2. Pin the fat quarters for the pockets, marked side up, to the interfacing; cut out the pockets from both layers.

3. Cut 4 pieces of ribbon, each 18" long.

sewing it up

Making the Pockets

1. Follow the manufacturer's instructions to fuse the interfacing pieces to the exterior and lining cover pieces and both pockets.

2. To hem both pockets, fold 1" to the wrong side along the longer top edge, press, fold down 1" again, and press again to enclose the raw edges. Edgestitch along the bottom fold.

3. Place the small pocket on the large pocket, both right sides up, aligning them at the bottom. Pin and machine baste them along the sides and bottom to make a pocket unit.

4. On the right side of the pocket unit, use a ruler and a disappearing-ink marker to draw a vertical line 2" in from the left edge of the small pocket *only*. Draw 3 additional vertical lines, each 1½" further in.

5. Stitch through both pocket layers on the lines drawn in Step 4, backstitching at the top of

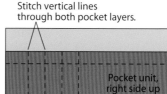

Stitch vertical lines through both pocket layers.

Pocket unit, right side up

2" 1½" 1½"1½"

the small pocket, to create slim channels on the smaller pocket. These will keep scissors and pens corralled neatly, while the wider pocket is perfect for a commercial pattern envelope.

Making the Cover

1. Layer the fused interior and exterior cover pieces, both right sides out, and place the pocket unit, right side up, at the bottom front of the exterior cover. Match up all the corners and pin together around the edges.

2. On the exterior side of the cover, pin the 18″ pieces of ribbon to the top of the small pocket on either side and 5″ from each end as shown, aligning the raw edges.

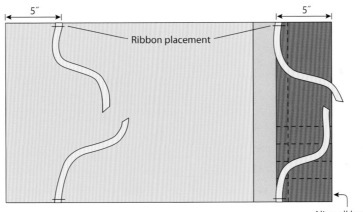

5″ Ribbon placement 5″

Align all layers at this end.

3. Refer to Bias Tape (page 17) to sandwich the double-fold bias tape around the outer edge of the cover, starting at what will be the back of the cover, where a ribbon is pinned. Edgestitch the bias tape in place, referring to *faux mitered corners* (page 17, in Bias Tape) to miter the corners. Join the ends as desired.

4. Press the cover so that it's neat and tidy, folding the ribbons outward over the bias trim. Pin and stitch the ribbons down on top of the edge stitching on the bias trim.

Now you have a pretty and protective cover to entice you back to your next sewing project!

sewing supply case

Finished size: closed—18″ × 20″; open—18″ × 36″

This supply case is a great way to stay organized at home or while crafting on the fly. I love this because it folds up neatly for storage or travel, but when I want to work from my home studio, I can hang it up on my pretty hook and get to sewing. Now all my sewing tools are in one space.

Materials and Supplies

2 yards midweight home decor fabric

1½ yards lightweight woven fusible interfacing, such as Shape-Flex by C&T Publishing

1¼ yards double-sided fusible stiff interfacing, such as fast2fuse Light by C&T Publishing

½ yard 1″-wide elastic

2 packages (or 8 yards) of purchased ½″-wide double-fold bias tape

¾ yard 1″-wide webbing

1 yard 1½″-wide webbing

1 magnetic snap

cutting it out

Making Patterns

Use a clear, gridded ruler and a pencil to measure the pieces. This sort of ruler, used by quilters, can help you create square corners. Mark each interfacing and fabric piece on the wrong side with its corresponding letter to keep track of them. Use a rotary cutter and mat to cut out the pieces quickly and easily.

Lightweight Woven Fusible Interfacing

1. Draw the following pieces on the nonfusible side of the interfacing as shown in the diagram (page 159). Do *not* cut them apart yet.

3 rectangles 5″ × 18″ for pocket A

1 rectangle 3″ × 18″ for pocket B

2 rectangles 8″ × 18″ for pocket C

1 rectangle 5″ × 14″ for pocket D

1 rectangle 3″ × 14″ for pocket E

1 rectangle 8″ × 18″ for pocket F

2. From remaining scrap of interfacing, cut 1 rectangle 3″ × 12″ for tab G.

Double-Sided Stiff Fusible Interfacing

Cut 1 rectangle 18″ × 39″ for the main panel.

Home Decor Fabric

1. Cut 2 rectangles 18″ × 39″ for the inner and outer main panels.

2. Cut 1 rectangle 21″ × 43″ for the pockets.

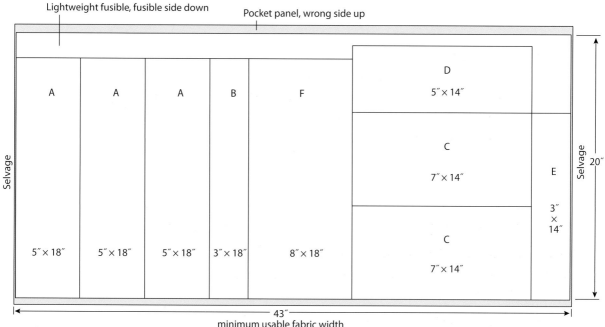

Lightweight fusible, fusible side down

Pocket panel, wrong side up

Selvage

Selvage

20″

A	A	A	B	F	D 5″ × 14″	
5″ × 18″	5″ × 18″	5″ × 18″	3″ × 18″	8″ × 18″	C 7″ × 14″	E 3″ × 14″
					C 7″ × 14″	

43″
minimum usable fabric width

Interfacing layout

fusing it

1. Following the manufacturer's instructions, fuse the large marked pocket interfacing piece onto the wrong side of the 21″ × 43″ piece of home decor fabric. Fuse the 3″ × 12″ tab interfacing to a remaining scrap of home decor fabric. Use a pressing cloth to protect the iron and ironing surface.

2. Cut out all the fused pockets and the snap tab on the drawn lines.

3. Fuse a main fabric panel to the stiff double-sided fusible. Make sure to follow the manufacturer's instructions; this interfacing is fusible on both sides, so you need to iron using parchment paper under the fusible so that it will not end up stuck to the ironing table.

4. The main panel gets a lot of manhandling during assembly, so reinforce the fusible interfacing by basting the 2 pieces together ⅛″ from the outer edges.

sewing it up

Preparing the Pockets

Refer to Bias Tape (page 17) to trim the top, wide edge of pockets A, B, D, E, and F with the double-fold bias tape, edgestitching it in place. Cut the tape flush with the sides of each pocket.

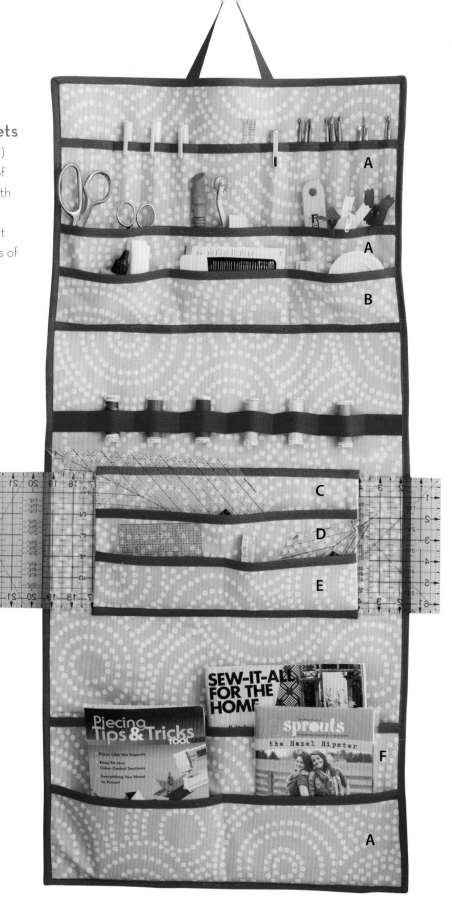

Section 1

1. On the right side of a pocket A piece, use a disappearing-ink marker to draw vertical lines spaced 1½" apart across the width of the pocket.

2. Position the marked pocket 3" down from the top of the fused main panel, both right sides up. Pin it in place and sew the bottom of the pocket to the main panel using a ¼" seam allowance.

3. Stitch on the lines that you drew in Step 1, making sure to backstitch at the top of each pocket for strength; you don't want all your hard work to fall apart. These slim pocket slots are great for small tools.

4. Layer pocket B on top of another pocket A, aligning and pinning them together at the bottom. We'll call this the A/B pocket unit. Sandwich and edgestitch the bottom edge of the A/B pocket unit with the bias tape, trimming the bias tape flush with the pocket sides.

5. With the disappearing-ink marker, draw 2 vertical lines 6" in from the sides of the A/B pocket unit, starting at the top of pocket A.

6. Place the A/B pocket unit, right side up, 7" down from the top edge of the fused main panel, just covering the bottom of the first A pocket. Pin in place along the sides and bottom of the unit. Edgestitch along the bottom of the bias tape to attach the pocket. Baste the sides of the pockets in place.

7. Stitch along the 2 lines drawn in Step 5, again making sure to backstitch at the top of the pocket for added strength, to create 3 pockets across the panel.

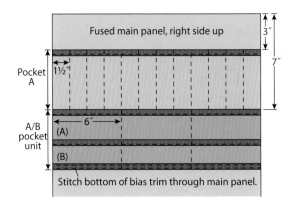

Section 2

1. Pin the 18″ piece of 1″-wide elastic across the fused main panel 4″ below the bottom of the A/B pocket unit. Use tailor's chalk to draw a line in the center of the elastic, and then draw 3 lines on either side of the center, each 2¼″ further out. Triple-stitch the elastic in place from top to bottom at the chalk marks. This elastic will snugly hold your thread spools.

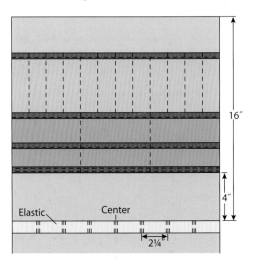

2. Layer pocket E onto pocket D, both right sides up, aligning them at the bottom. Pin them together. Use the disappearing-ink marker to draw a 3″ line down the center of pocket E. Stitch the 2 pockets together along this line, backstitching at the top, dividing pocket E into 2 sections.

3. Place the D/E pocket unit on top of a pocket C, both right sides up, aligning them at the bottom. Pin together along the bottom and baste together along the sides and the bottom, using a ¼″ seam allowance. We'll call this pocket unit C/D/E.

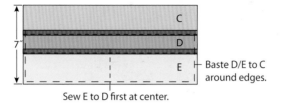

Sew E to D first at center.

4. The C/D/E pocket unit is left open on the sides instead of at the top so that a large clear ruler can slide in and out easily. To finish the pocket, pin the remaining pocket C to the C/D/E unit, right sides together, along the 7″ sides. Sew both of the 7″ sides together using a ½″ seam allowance.

5. Turn the pocket right side out and press the seams flat. Baste the top and bottom of the pocket C/D/E unit closed, using a ¼″ seam allowance.

6. Trim the top and bottom of the unit with bias tape, referring to Bias Tape (page 17) to finish the ends by tucking them into the back side of the bias tape.

7. Pin the C/D/E pocket 1½″ down from the bottom edge of the elastic, centered from side to side.

8. Edgestitch the pocket at the top and bottom on the outer edges of the bias trim to attach it to the main panel. Reinforce the beginning and end of each seam with a second line of stitching 1″ long.

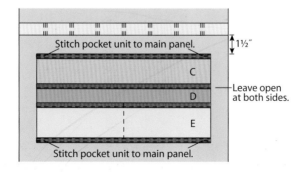

Section 3

1. Pin the remaining pocket A onto pocket F, both right sides up, aligning the bottom corners. With the disappearing-ink marker, draw a vertical line down the center of pocket A. Stitch along this line, again backstitching at the top of the pocket for added strength.

2. Align the bottom of pocket unit F/A at the bottom of the main panel. Pin and baste the pocket in place ¼″ from the bottom and sides of the pocket/panel.

Handles and Snap

1. Fold snap tab G in half lengthwise, right sides together, as shown. Draw a line across the width 1″ away from the fold line and then draw another that crosses it at the center, thus marking the center of the magnetic snap.

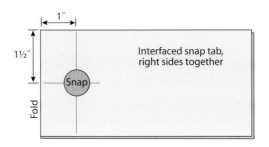

2. Place the metal plate that came with the magnetic snap on the tab, centering the plate on the center mark from the previous step. Trace inside the openings and then cut the slits open and follow the manufacturer's instructions to insert the male side of the snap.

3. After the snap is securely positioned, refold the snap tab, right sides together again, and then sew the sides closed using a ½″ seam allowance. Clip the corners and turn the tab right side out; use a point turner or chopstick to get the corners nice and crisp. Press and set it aside.

4. From the 1½″-wide webbing, cut 2 pieces, each 18″ long. Sew a tight zigzag stitch at the ends of the cut webbing to keep them from unraveling.

5. For the handles, cut the 1″-wide webbing into 2 pieces, each 13″ long. Again, sew a tight zigzag stitch at each end of the webbing.

6. Mark the center on the wrong side of each of the 1½″ webbing pieces. Mark 2″ out from either side of the center.

7. Pin the 1″-wide webbing handles to the wider webbing pieces outside the 2″ marks, ½″ down from the top edge of the wider webbing, to make 4″-wide handle loops.

8. Pin the snap tab to 1 piece of the wider webbing, matching the centers, placing the raw edge of the snap tab 1″ down from the top edge of the webbing as shown. Add the other side of the magnetic snap to the center of the other webbing handle as shown. Make sure your snap tabs are placed so that they will meet up when the supply case is closed.

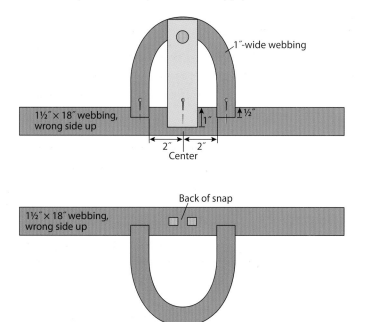

9. Sew the handles and the snap tab into place along the edge of the wider webbing.

Case Backing

1. On the right side of the remaining main panel, draw a horizontal line 1½″ from the top with a disappearing-ink marker. Mark the center of the panel along this line.

2. Repeat Step 1, but 14″ from the bottom.

3. Pin the 2 handle webbing units below the 1½″ line and above the 14″ line as shown. Edgestitch in place.

4. Following the manufacturer's instructions, fuse the back main panel to the double fusible side of the main panel with the pockets. The webbing with the female snap tab should be at the A/A/B end of the outer main panel.

Trim

With the pocket side of the case up, sandwich the raw edges of the case within the double-fold bias tape, starting with the edge of the bias trim flush with the bottom right corner. Refer to Bias Tape (page 17) to

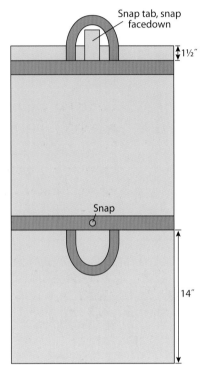

Snap tab, snap facedown

1½″

Snap

14″

pin and edgestitch the bias trim in place: Refer to *faux mitered corners* to turn the corners. When you reach the starting point, refer to *overlap fold finish* to carefully tuck the bias over the corner and back into the fold of the bias.

Load up your new sewing supply case as you clean up. Sewing never looked so organized.

embroidered pincushion

Finished size: 4½" wide × 3" long × 1½" deep

Everyone needs a good pincushion! A little embroidery makes this one extra special. A few simple stitches are all you need to know; it's a fast and easy introduction into a relaxing new hobby.

Materials and Supplies

1 fat quarter of calico

Scrap of wool felt

Perle cotton #8 and embroidery floss in colors to coordinate with the calico

Small piece of tissue paper

Small embroidery hoop

Pattern

1. Trace or copy pincushion pattern on page 171.

2. Take a piece of tissue paper slightly larger than the design and place it on top of the embroidery design on page 171. With a fine-tip marker, trace the design onto the tissue paper. You'll be embroidering through it onto the felt.

Fabric

1. Cut the calico in half lengthwise; then trace the pincushion pattern on the wrong side of the fabric. Do not cut out your pincushion at this time.

2. Cut 1 rectangle 2½" × 3½" from the wool felt.

embroidering it up

For instructions on making the stitches, see page 172.

1. Flip your calico to the wrong side, where the grain is more easily seen. *The felt must be situated parallel to the grain of the cotton fabric.* For more on grain, refer to *grain* (page 15, in Tips and Tricks). Trace the felt rectangle on the center of the wrong side of the calico and then use a few pins to mark the corners. Pin the felt rectangle onto the front, using the corner pins for placement.

2. Hand baste the felt to the calico and remove any pins.

3. Pin and then hand baste the tissue paper to the felt. Use the corners on the design to position it on the felt correctly.

4. Beginning with the flowers in the corners, stitch lazy-daisy petals for all the flowers. Use a single strand of #8 perle cotton or 3 strands of floss. Mine were a cheery yellow.

5. For the vines and leaves, use 4 strands of floss—I used green. Split stitch the vines and stitch lazy daisies for the leaves.

6. Using 1 strand of perle cotton, make French knots in the center of each lazy-daisy flower and between the 2 leaves in the corner with the extra vine.

7. Remove the tissue paper from the stitches slowly and carefully. Use tweezers or the tip of a stiletto to remove any hard-to-reach or stubborn tissue.

sewing it up

1. Fold the embroidered fabric in half, right sides together, and cut out the 2 pieces of the pincushion on the traced pattern lines.

2. Pin the 2 pieces, right sides together, and sew both of the short sides together from end to end with a ¼" seam allowance. Sew a long side together from end to end, and on the other long side leave a 2" opening to turn the pincushion right side out later.

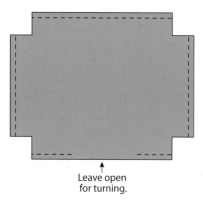

Leave open
for turning.

3. To sew the corners, pull the layers of fabric apart from each other and pinch the width and length seams together so that they match.

Pin them together, making sure that the seams are opposite each other. In other words, you want the width seam allowance going up and the length going down. Repeat on all 4 corners.

4. Sew the corners together using a ¼" seam allowance.

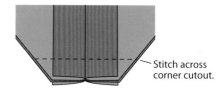

Stitch across
corner cutout.

5. Turn the cushion right side out and stuff with polyester fiberfill until it's firm—but not over-stuffed. Fold the seam allowances in at the side opening and pin it shut. Refer to Hand Stitches (page 172) to slipstitch the seam shut.

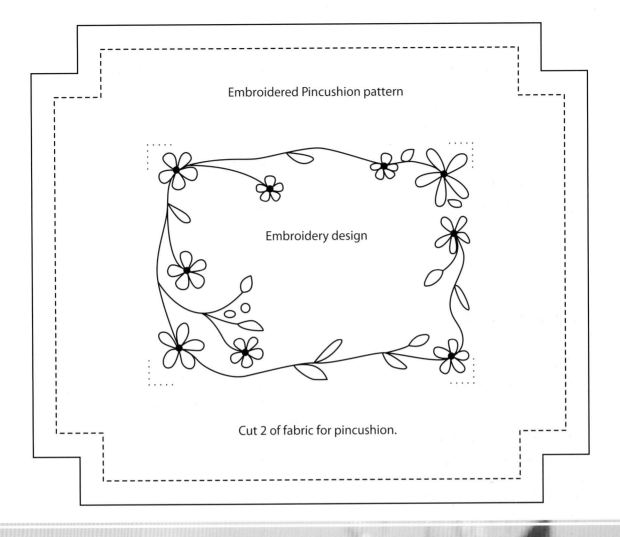

Embroidered Pincushion pattern

Embroidery design

Cut 2 of fabric for pincushion.

Now you have a pretty and safe place to store your pins and needles for your next project.

French Knot

1. With a single strand of perle cotton, bring the needle up from the wrong side of the fabric at A. Keep the thread taut with a thumb while wrapping it around the needle 2 times (or 3 times for my "candy knot") with your other hand.

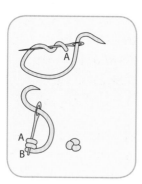

2. Still holding the thread with your thumb, twist the needle back to the starting point (A), and insert it close to where the thread emerged (B). The stitch needs a few bits of fabric to grab onto, so avoid going into the same hole.

3. Pull the needle through the wrapped perle cotton and fabric toward the back while firmly holding the knotted thread close to the fabric. Let go when the loops are nearly closed to form the knot.

Lazy Daisy

1. Bring the needle from the wrong side to the right side of the fabric (A). Then take the needle to the back, as close as possible to where the thread emerges, leaving a loop of thread on top of the fabric (B). Bring the needle up again at the tip of the stitch (C), looping the thread counterclockwise around the needle tip. Use your thumb to keep the thread from twisting while pulling the needle through to the wrong side of the fabric (D).

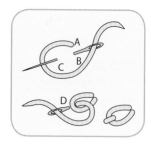

2. Move on to the next petal, adjacent to where you started the first.

Running Stitch

Start by threading your needle and knotting off the end. From the wrong side of the fabric, come up in the center of a square along the right side (A). Place the needle through to the wrong side of the fabric (B) and bring it back up to the top side (C). Repeat.

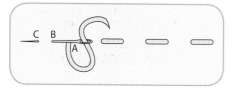

Slip Stitch

1. Take a tiny stitch in the fabric.

2. Insert the point of the needle in the fold of the hem and slip along inside the fold for ¼" or less.

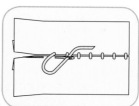

3. Pull the needle out, and take another tiny stitch in the fabric.

4. Repeat Steps 2 and 3.

Snowflake Stitch

Also known as a double cross-stitch.

1. Thread a needle and knot the thread. Make a cross-stitch by coming up from the bottom from A to B and then from C to D. Continue to make another cross over the first by bringing the needle out through E.

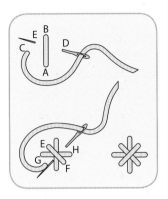

2. Now go from E to F and then from G to H. Without knotting off, move on to the next snowflake stitch, moving counterclockwise in the design.

Split Stitch

1. Thread your needle with 3–4 strands of embroidery floss and knot off the ends. Come up at A and make a small stitch about ¼" long (B).

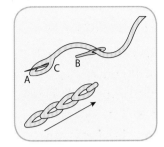

2. Next, bring your needle up through the center of the stitch you just made (C). Come down again as you did with your first stitch, and repeat. Continue with every stitch that follows, coming up through the last stitch you made.

Woven Circle Stitch

This combination is usually stitched on gingham, which provides spacing for the pattern based on the light and dark squares in the gingham weave. Each different stitch can be done in a different color, or only the woven circle itself can be made in a different color.

1. Make 2 rows of 2 snowflake stitches, each separated by a gingham square.

2. Stitch a single running stitch on each square between each pair of snowflake stitches.

3. Bring the needle to the front at the inside of a running stitch and wrap the thread around the inside ends of all 4 running stitches, twice, to create a circle. Bring the needle down through your starting point.

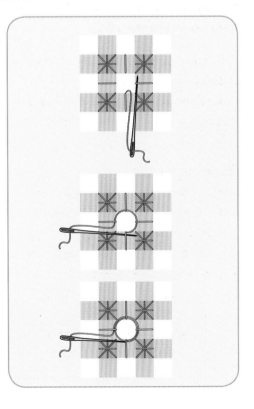

BIBLIOGRAPHY

Resources

Oilcloth, laminated cotton, and chalk cloth

modernjune.com

Ideas, projects, and materials

Timtex, Shape-Flex, fast2fuse, Insul-Fleece, and Alex Anderson's 4-in-1 Essential Sewing Tool

ctpub.com

Vintage Pot Holders

Find these at your local thrift or antique stores, estate sales, or online at etsy.com.

Cozy cottons

citycraftonline.com

modernjune.spoonflower.com

projectanthologies.com

sewfabulousquiltshop.com

Buttons and Ribbons

Riley Blake Designs, available at modernjune.com and at many local quilt shops nationwide.

Becker, Holly, Joanna Copestick, and Debi Treloar. *Decorate: 1,000 Professional Design Ideas for Every Room in Your Home.* San Francisco: Chronicle, 2011. Print.

Becker, Holly, and Debi Treloar. *Decorate Workshop: Design and Style Your Space in Eight Creative Steps.* San Francisco: Chronicle, 2012. Print.

Blondin, Frances. *The New Encyclopedia of Modern Sewing.* New York: W.H. Wise & Co., 1946. Print.

Hartman, Elizabeth. *The Practical Guide to Patchwork: New Basics for the Modern Quiltmaker—12 Quilt Projects.* Lafayette, CA: Stash, 2010. Print.

Latour, Laurie. *Guide to Gingham Embroidery: Book One.* Honea Path, S.C.: Marmee Dear & Co., 2011. E-book. marmeedearandcompany.com/shoppe > Laurie Latour > Gingham Embroidery > Guide to Gingham Embroidery.

McCall's Home Fashion Sew-It Book: The Home Decorator's Guide for Creative Sewing. New York: McCall, 1965. Print.

McCants, Kelly. *Sewing with Oilcloth: 20 Patterns That Make Sewing with Oilcloth Easy, Fresh, and Fun.* Hoboken, N.J.: John Wiley & Sons, 2011. Print.

Sew-It-All for the Home: Simplicity's How-To Book of Sewing with Decorator Patterns. New York: Simplicity Pattern Co., 1973. Print.

Stewart, Martha. *Martha Stewart's Encyclopedia of Sewing and Fabric Crafts: Basic Techniques for Sewing, Appliqué, Embroidery, Quilting, Dyeing, and Printing.* New York: Potter Craft, 2010. Print.

ABOUT THE AUTHOR

Kelly McCants, a.k.a. Modern June, the Oilcloth Addict, learned to sew at age thirteen and has spent a lifetime stitching and drafting patterns. In college, she studied costume design and worked in film and theater costume shops all over the United States until she became a mother of two.

The McCants family lives in an 87-year-old house in a charming neighborhood in Richmond, Virginia. During their early years of parenthood, Kelly and her husband, Don, spent a lot of time restoring the house.

In 2006, Kelly began homeschooling her children and started her company, Modern June, as a creative outlet. Her hand-sewn housewares business grew as quickly as the kids, with everything happening in her home until early 2013, when Modern June moved to a nearby studio space. She maintains a home studio and says it's a creative place of peace—if you don't mind the teenagers!

Kelly wrote *Sewing with Oilcloth* in 2011 and actively writes two blogs, Modern June (modernjune.blogspot.com) and Oilcloth Addict (oilclothaddict.blogspot.com). Kelly sells fabric, notions, and her own line of hand-sewn housewares on etsy.com and at modernjune.com.

The projects in this book grew out of Kelly's whole-house makeover—her second one in fourteen years. She's proud to share it all with you.